LEARNING THROUGH LITERATURE

Projects and Activities for Linking Literature and Writing

W9-AWY-965

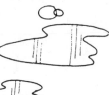

by Denise Bieniek, M.S.
Illustrated by Wayne Becker

Troll!

CREATIVE
TEACHER
IDEAS

Troll Creative Teacher Ideas was designed to help today's dedicated, time-pressured teacher. Created by teachers for teachers, this innovative series provides a wealth of classroom ideas to help reinforce important concepts and stimulate your students' creative thinking skills.

Each book in the series focuses on a different curriculum theme to give you the flexibility to teach any given skill at any time of the year. The wide range of ideas and activities included in each book are certain to help you create an atmosphere where students are continually eager to learn new concepts and develop important skills.

We hope this comprehensive series will provide you with everything you need to foster a fun and challenging learning environment for your students. **Troll Creative Teacher Ideas** is a resource you'll turn to again and again!

Titles in this series:

Classroom Decor:
Decorate Your Classroom from Bulletin Boards to Time Lines

Creative Projects: Quick and Easy Art Projects

Earth Alert: Environmental Studies for Grades 4-6

Explore the World: Social Studies Projects and Activities

Healthy Bodies, Healthy Minds

Holidays Around the World: Multicultural Projects and Activities

It All Adds Up: Math Skill-Building Activities for Grades 4-6

Learning Through Literature:
Projects and Activities for Linking Literature and Writing

Story Writing: Creative Writing Projects and Activities

Think About It: Skill-Building Puzzles Across the Curriculum

The World Around Us: Geography Projects and Activities

World Explorers: Discover the Past

Metric Conversion Chart

1 inch = 2.54 cm	1 foot = .305 m	1 yard = .914 m
1 mile = 1.61 km	1 fluid ounce = 29.573 ml	1 cup = .24 l
1 pint = .473 l	1 teaspoon = 4.93 ml	1 tablespoon = 14.78 ml

10 9 8 7 6 5 4 3 2

Contents

Then and Now Bulletin Board

Ask students to read *Little House in the Big Woods* by Laura Ingalls Wilder. As they read, ask the children to make notes in journals or on note pads about life in pioneer times: food, housing, recreation, transportation, and communication.

When students come together in groups or as a class to discuss the book, have them compare their notes. Talk about how the land where the Ingalls family lived was surrounded by forests and was a place where wild animals roamed; how the family obtained their food by growing crops, hunting, and fishing; the types of toys with which the children played (pig's bladder, rag dolls, and corncob dolls); the types of transportation used (horses, wagon, bobsled); and their methods of heating, lighting, and cooking (fireplace, kerosene lamps, and wood stove).

Ask students to compare and contrast life in pioneer times with those of today. Have them list what they have in their homes for cooking and heating, what types of transportation they use, and how they like to spend their free time.

Divide a bulletin board in half and back each side with a different-colored paper. Title one side "Pioneer Days" and the other "Nowadays." Ask students to write about and illustrate what life was like back in pioneer times and what life is like today. Staple their work on the appropriate half of the board.

Take a Good Look

Name

Read the following passages from *Little House in the Big Woods* by Laura Ingalls Wilder. On a separate piece of paper, write down a description of a similar event from your own life. For example, one of the passages is about relatives coming to visit the Ingalls' at Christmas time. You may wish to write about traveling to visit relatives or friends during a holiday celebration.

The great, dark trees of the Big Woods stood all around the house, and beyond them were other trees and beyond them were more trees. As far as a man could go to the north in a day, or a week, or a whole month, there was nothing but woods.

The day before Christmas they came. Laura and Mary heard the gay ringing of sleigh bells, growing louder every moment, and then the big bobsled came out of the woods and drove up to the gate. Aunt Eliza and Uncle Peter and the cousins were in it, all covered up, under blankets and robes and buffalo skins.

Laura asked him how he got the honey away from the bees. "That was easy," Pa said. "I left the horses back in the woods, where they wouldn't get stung, and then I chopped the tree down and split it open."
"Didn't the bees sting you?"
"No," said Pa. "Bees never sting me."

Advice Column

Let students try out their abilities to give advice. Begin an advice column based on any troubles the Ingalls or one of their family members may be experiencing. The problem may even be one a student has with a particular chapter or a passage in the story that they do not understand.

Ask students to identify a problem one of the characters may be having. For example, on the day the Ingalls go to Pepin, Laura is under the impression that brown hair is ugly and blond hair is much prettier. A student may wish to pretend to be Laura and write a letter complaining that she has ugly brown hair and how that makes her feel. (Students should not use their real names when they sign their letters.)

Then have students place their letters in a bag. Mix up the letters and ask each child to pick a letter from the bag. Tell students that they should try to think of advice to give to the authors of the letters. Students may want to bring the letters home in order to have time to think about what they will write.

Attach the letters to a bulletin board for all to see. Title the board "Old-Time Advice."

Who Said It?

Name _____

Try to identify which of the *Little House in the Big Woods* characters is speaking in each of these passages.

When I went to town yesterday with the furs I found it hard walking in the soft snow. It took me a long time to get to town, and other men with furs had come in earlier to do their trading. The storekeeper was busy, and I had to wait until he could look at my furs.

Speaker: _____

His tracks were the biggest I ever saw. He would have got Eliza sure, if Prince had let her go to the spring in the morning. He had been lying up in that big oak tree over the spring, waiting for some animal to come there for water.

Speaker: _____

I don't care. Aunt Lotty likes my hair best, anyway. Golden hair is lots prettier than brown.

Speaker: _____

Sukey is safe in the barn. Think, Laura—all those big, heavy logs in the barn walls. And the door is heavy and solid, made to keep bears out. No, the bear cannot get in and eat Sukey.

Speaker: _____

Is the moon really made of green cheese?

Speaker: _____

Little House Trivia

Name _____

Do you remember these parts of *Little House in the Big Woods*? Circle the correct answer to each question.

1. Who came to visit the Ingalls family for Christmas?
- **A.** Aunt Eliza and Uncle Peter
- **B.** Grandpa
- **C.** the Petersons
- **D.** Aunt Ruby and Aunt Docia

2. What did the storekeeper give to Laura and Mary?
- **A.** Calico fabric
- **B.** Candy
- **C.** Bread and butter and cheese
- **D.** Toys

3. What rule did Grandpa break when he went out on the sled with his brothers?
- **A.** No sled riding during a snowstorm.
- **B.** Only one person may ride on the sled at a time.
- **C.** Finish the chores before playing.
- **D.** No sled riding on Sundays.

4. What was rennet used for?
- **A.** Cleaning
- **B.** Making cheese
- **C.** Traveling
- **D.** Making furniture

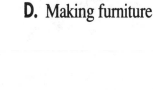

5. What happened to Charley when he didn't help harvest the oats?
- **A.** He was sent to bed without supper.
- **B.** He had to work all day Saturday.
- **C.** He was stung by yellow jackets.
- **D.** He was chased by a bear.

On a separate piece of paper, tell about your favorite part of the book. Who is your favorite character, and why?

Lost and Found Posters

MATERIALS:

crayons or markers
paint and paintbrushes
poster paper or oaktag

DIRECTIONS:

1. Ask each student to choose his or her favorite animal character from *Charlotte's Web*. Tell the children to make lost and found posters for the characters. Distribute poster paper or oaktag along with crayons, markers, paint, and paintbrushes to students.

2. Ask students what information a lost and found poster should contain, such as the name of the animal, its home address and phone number, a description of the animal, and where it was last seen. They may also wish to draw a picture of the animal.

3. When the posters are finished, ask students to read their posters, omitting the name of the animal characters. Then see if the class can figure out which animal each student is describing. Afterwards, students may wish to offer suggestions regarding information given which would help better describe the various characters.

4. Hang the posters around the room. After the class has finished reading the book, allow students to take their posters home.

Pet Survey

MATERIALS:

paper
clipboard or other hard writing surface
pens

DIRECTIONS:

1. Help students make up a questionnaire to be answered by other students in their school. The survey's goal is to discover which pets most students wish they could have.

2. A few background questions, such as student's sex and grade level, will help when analyzing the results later. Explain to the class that survey analysts use this information to categorize groups of people, making results easier to graph and read.

3. The survey question should come next: If you could choose any animal for a pet, which one would it be? Survey makers might also ask the question: Why did you choose the animal you did?

4. Distribute the surveys to the other classes in the same grade level as well as one or two classes from different grade levels. Ask the teachers of the classes chosen for the survey when it would be convenient to have students fill in the surveys.

5. Tally the results under categories chosen by the students. If they choose to use Boy/Girl categories, they would write the animal most boys chose and the animal that the girls chose most frequently. Or they could divide the results between the grade levels of those taking the survey: 4th Grade/ 5th Grade/ 6th Grade. Another way to categorize is by naming the ten most popular pets and how many students named that animal.

6. Students may represent the information in many forms: bar graphs, pie charts, and line graphs.

7. Share the results with the classes involved in the survey.

Ode to Charlotte

Ask students what it was that made Wilbur and Charlotte such good friends. Then ask what they think Wilbur was thinking when he found out Charlotte was going to die, and how he was able to go on remembering Charlotte after her death.

Explain to the class that other ways of remembering people or animals after they have died is to write an ode, obituary, or epitaph about them. Ask if anyone can define one of the words. (*Ode* means a poem, rhymed or unrhymed, to some person or thing; *obituary* means a notice of someone's death, usually with a short biography; *epitaph* means an inscription on a tomb or gravestone in memory of the person buried there.)

Ask students to write one of the forms of tribute listed above as though they were Wilbur writing about Charlotte. They may emphasize different aspects about her: she was a spider, her web-making, how she made Wilbur safe for the rest of his life, their unique friendship, or her offspring and the future generations that stay with Wilbur.

Encourage students to share their tributes to Charlotte with the class. Attach the tributes to a classroom wall or a bulletin board for all to see.

Name _____

Put the following events from *Charlotte's Web* in the order in which they happen in the story. Write a number in each blank space.

_____ Wilbur goes to the fair.

_____ Charlotte and Wilbur meet.

_____ Charlotte's children come to live with Wilbur.

_____ Fern saves Wilbur from being killed.

_____ Wilbur goes to live with the Zuckermans.

_____ Charlotte lays her eggs.

_____ Charlotte writes "SOME PIG" in her web.

_____ Wilbur gets a buttermilk bath.

_____ Charlotte writes "TERRIFIC" in her web.

_____ Wilbur escapes from the yard.

Book Jacket

MATERIALS:

12" x 18" paper
pens and pencils
crayons or markers
paints or watercolors and paintbrushes
pastels or chalk

DIRECTIONS:

1. Ask students to create book jackets for *Where the Red Fern Grows* after completing the book. Distribute 12" x 18" paper and writing tools to students. Demonstrate how to fold the paper into a book jacket: fold the paper 4" in on each short side, then again in half so the first folds meet.

2. Ask the children what they might expect to find on a book jacket. Then ask each student to design a book jacket that shows an illustration of one of the events in the book on the cover, the title and author, and a blurb about the book that will catch a reader's attention and make him or her want to read the book. The student may also write a short paragraph about the author for the inside back flap of the jacket.

3. Stand the book jackets up on cabinets and counter tops so everyone in the class may read how others interpreted the book. Discuss the different events and themes of the story students chose to highlight and why.

Where the RED FERN grows

by Wilson Rawls

What's the Question? Game

As a review of *Where the Red Fern Grows*, play the following game with the class. You will need four panelists, an announcer, and writers. Choose the four panelists first. The announcer and writers will make up questions and answers based on facts in *Where the Red Fern Grows*. At this time, panelists may wish to review the story.

The writers should fold 5" x 7" index cards in half and write answers to questions on the inside of each card. Writers should then write a number from 1 to 4 on the front of each folded index card (easier questions should be numbered "1," and the hardest questions should be numbered "4"). The announcer should then copy down all the answers along with their corresponding questions on another sheet of paper. When questions and answers are ready, the writers should put them into four categories. Tape labels for each

category on the chalkboard or wall, then tape the folded index cards under the appropriate category.

Bring in the panelists and announcer. The oldest player goes first, and the youngest goes last. The announcer calls out the categories chosen for the game and asks each player in turn to pick a category and number card. Then the announcer turns over the chosen card and the panelist asks a question that will fit the answer written on it. The announcer can check the list he or she made to make sure the question is correct.

If a panelist makes up a question for an answer correctly, he or she wins the number of points written on the front of the answer card. If a panelist cannot make up an appropriate question, the next panelist gets a chance to answer and may go again until stumped.

When all the cards have been used, the panelist with the most points wins.

Pet Talk

Ask students to describe a pet they have at home or a pet they wish they could have, without mentioning the name of the animal. See how many students can guess the animal when the speaker is done describing it.

Then tell students that they will be making a speech to the class about a pet. The speech should be two minutes or less. The content may be about an adventure they had with a pet, how the pet was originally obtained, what the pet and owner like to do, special tricks, or the unique personality a pet may have.

The speech may be a real story or a made-up one. It should be convincing enough so that students are guessing at the end whether the story is real or not.

Set up one day a week for several weeks on which students may bring in their pets from home to show to the rest of the class. Tell students to show off any tricks, special talents, or features that their pets have.

Descriptively Speaking

Name _____

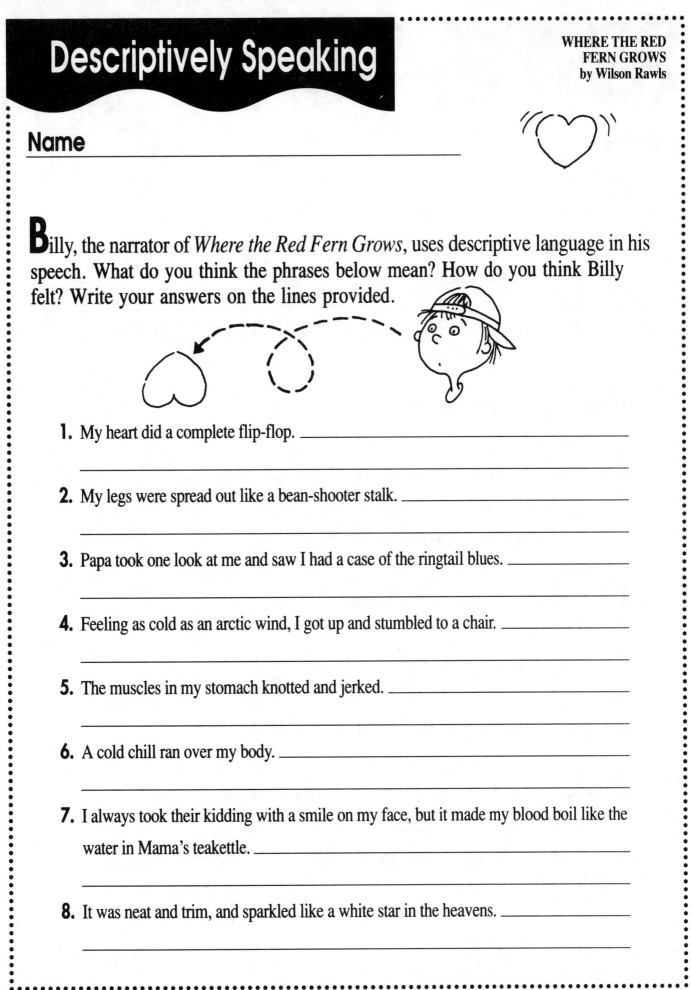

Billy, the narrator of *Where the Red Fern Grows*, uses descriptive language in his speech. What do you think the phrases below mean? How do you think Billy felt? Write your answers on the lines provided.

1. My heart did a complete flip-flop. _____

    _____

2. My legs were spread out like a bean-shooter stalk. _____

    _____

3. Papa took one look at me and saw I had a case of the ringtail blues. _____

    _____

4. Feeling as cold as an arctic wind, I got up and stumbled to a chair. _____

    _____

5. The muscles in my stomach knotted and jerked. _____

    _____

6. A cold chill ran over my body. _____

    _____

7. I always took their kidding with a smile on my face, but it made my blood boil like the

    water in Mama's teakettle. _____

    _____

8. It was neat and trim, and sparkled like a white star in the heavens. _____

    _____

Homonym Search

Name _____

A **homonym** is one of two or more words that sound the same, and sometimes have the same spellings, but have different meanings.

Circle the homonyms in these sentences from *Where the Red Fern Grows*. Then write a homonym and its definition for each word in the spaces provided.

1. She looked as if she were asleep but I knew she wasn't.

   _____

2. I cocked my ear to see if I could hear puppies crying, but could hear nothing.

   _____

3. I had lost weight and was as thin as a bean pole.

   _____

4. You should have seen what I saw one day.

   _____

5. I kept it up for the rest of the night.

   _____

6. I felt so good even my sore hands had stopped hurting.

   _____

7. His tail was between his legs and his head was bowed down.

   _____

8. Just before he drew one last sigh, and a feeble thump of his tail, his friendly gray eyes closed forever.

   _____

Narnia Dioramas

MATERIALS:

shoe boxes
crayons or markers
construction paper
oaktag
scissors
collage materials
glue
natural objects (twigs, grass, rocks)

DIRECTIONS:

1. Discuss some of the different settings found in *The Lion, the Witch and the Wardrobe*, i.e., London during wartime with its bombed-out buildings, the Professor's big old house with the magic wardrobe, the lamppost in Narnia with snow falling and the faun standing with his packages, the White Witch and her castle, or Aslan surrounded by spring-time.

2. Ask each student to choose his or her favorite setting to use in making a diorama. Distribute shoe boxes and art materials to students and allow them time each day to work on their dioramas.

3. When the dioramas are finished, have students write short descriptions of their chosen settings, why they like them, and why these settings are important parts of the story.

4. Set up the dioramas on tables around the room and let students walk around the room to observe and read about the different settings.

Narnia Tours Travel Agency

MATERIALS:

crayons or markers
paints, watercolors, and paintbrushes
collage materials
glue
construction paper
pens

DIRECTIONS:

1. Tell the students that they are now travel agents for Narnia Tours Travel Agency. The boss has just announced that tourism has fallen off, and she wants new advertising campaigns letting people know more about Narnia and why it is a great place to visit.

2. Students may come up with their own strategies for the campaign: a television commercial, a radio blurb or a jingle, or a travel brochure. When students have come up with their strategies, allow them time to adapt their ideas onto paper.

3. Encourage students to share their campaigns with the class and tell how they came up with their ideas. Display the various ideas around the room for all to look at during free time.

4. As an extension activity, ask students to pretend that they have taken a trip to Narnia for the weekend. Have students write about their trips and make illustrations to go along with their stories.

NARNIA TOURS
TRAVEL AGENCY

Narnia Sculptures

MATERIALS:
flour
salt
water
paints and paintbrushes
shellac

DIRECTIONS:
1. Mix 2 cups of flour with 2 cups of salt. Add water and stir until the mixture becomes dough-like.
2. Students can choose their favorite characters from *The Lion, the Witch and the Wardrobe*, then use the clay they have made to mold figures of these characters. When the sculptures are finished, allow them to dry for two to three days.
3. Give students paints and paintbrushes to use to add details to their figures. A coating of shellac will help seal the finish.
4. When the sculptures have dried, students may display their figures and discuss why they chose that particular character. Then ask each child to give a short step-by-step speech telling the class how they formed the figure, any difficulties they may have had, or techniques that worked well for them. Keep the figures on display until the class has completed the book.

Map of Narnia

Name _____

Draw a map of what you imagine Narnia would look like. Try to include the lamppost, the sea, the White Witch's castle, the stone table, Cair Paravel, where the battle was fought, the beaver's house, the river, and Mr. Tumnus's cave.

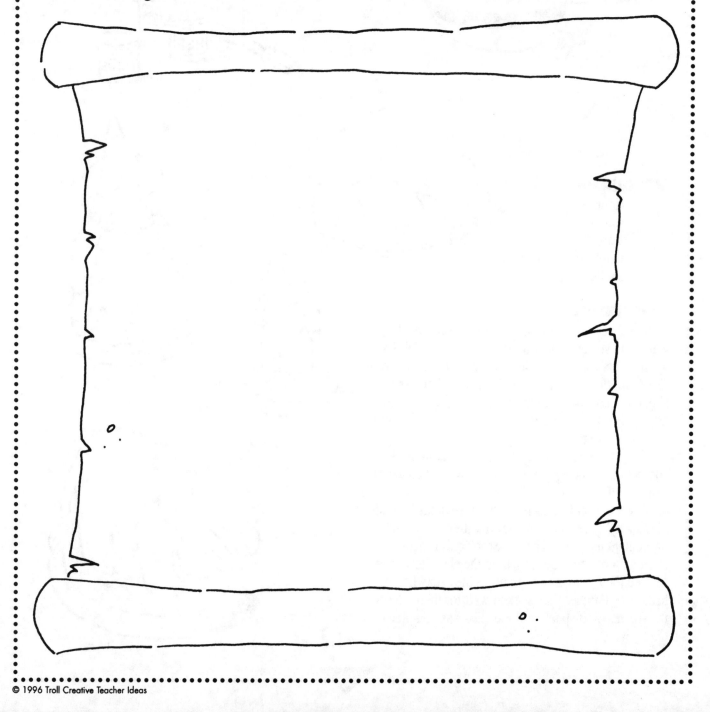

The Magic of Narnia

Name _____

On the lines below, answer two of the following questions after reading *The Lion, the Witch and the Wardrobe.*

1. Have you ever thought of a magical world like Narnia? Describe what this world might be like, and how you would get there.

2. Describe a talking animal that you would like to meet on a trip to Narnia.

3. What other sorts of magical gifts might have been useful for Peter, Susan, Edmund, and Lucy?

4. What might have happened if Peter, Susan, and Lucy had gone with Edmund to the White Witch's castle?

5. What would you change about the ending of the story?

_____

_____

_____

_____

_____

_____

_____

Mythical Creatures Word Search

Name _____

Circle the hidden words from *The Lion, the Witch and the Wardrobe*. The words may be written forward, backward, up, down, or diagonally.

```
S  I  N  C  S  P  E  C  T  R  E  W
P  O  F  R  K  Y  A  H  P  M  Y  N
R  U  A  T  O  N  I  M  N  I  M  A
I  D  U  I  N  C  U  B  E  T  T  I
T  U  N  I  C  O  R  N  R  P  S  A
E  E  U  J  O  E  S  O  O  W  B  D
B  T  J  A  V  G  N  F  T  Z  R  F
W  T  Z  S  T  K  R  T  L  Y  J  V
Y  I  X  L  H  O  L  F  A  U  Y  C
T  N  K  E  A  U  N  D  Z  U  N  R
E  Y  K  U  G  Q  N  I  O  G  R  E
E  R  W  R  A  I  G  I  M  I  Y  L
R  D  E  C  O  T  A  S  M  A  T  K
F  W  R  A  I  T  H  N  Y  W  A  R
E  S  U  B  U  C  N  I  T  Y  S  O
```

centaur	faun	naiad	nymph
satyr	giant	dryad	unicorn
ogre	cruel	hag	incubus
wraith	efreet	sprite	orkny
woos	ettin	minotaur	spectre

The Giant Fruit Book

MATERIALS:

- crayons or markers
- construction paper (smaller and larger sizes)
- scissors
- oaktag
- hole puncher
- yarn
- glue

DIRECTIONS:

1. Ask students to name other types of fruits besides peaches. Write their suggestions on the chalkboard or on a large piece of paper. Then ask each student to choose one of the fruits to illustrate.

2. Tell the class that they will each be making a book titled "The Giant Fruit," in which different fruits will hold various animals and people of their imaginings. Distribute paper and art materials.

3. Instruct students to make two cutouts of each piece of fruit. Each child should then glue the tops of the two layers together, leaving all the other edges free so the fruit may be opened to reveal the bottom layer.

4. On the bottom layer, each child should create creatures that will live inside the fruit as James and the insects did in *James and the Giant Peach*. The creatures may be imaginary or real, human or animal.

5. When the artwork is done, have each student glue the fruit onto a larger sheet of construction paper. Then ask each child to write about an adventure the creatures in the fruit share.

6. Cut two sheets of oaktag to the size of the larger sheets of construction paper to make a front and back cover. Punch three holes down the left side of the oaktag covers and the pages students made. Bind each book by tying yarn through the holes.

7. Students may wish to read the stories to younger classes during their free time.

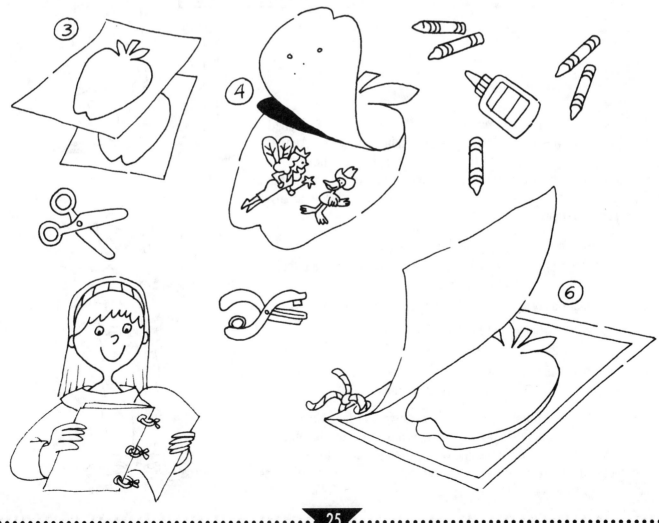

In the beginning of *James and the Giant Peach*, James is orphaned and forced to live with two maiden aunts, Aunt Sponge and Aunt Spiker. His life is miserable, for he is beaten and never allowed to play in the garden. After reading the beginning of the book have children form groups. Ask each group a different question listed below to answer in response journals.

What problem does the author use to get the story started?

Describe the relationship between the two aunts, then their relationship with James.

What idea or ideas does this chapter make you think about?

How does the author get you to think about them?

Who is the main character of the story?

What kind of person is he and what evidence is there in the chapter to support your judgments?

When students are finished writing their responses (during class time or as homework), ask them to discuss their answers with the other students in their group. At the end of group time, have students come together and let a speaker for each group share what the group's general consensus was about the question.

Character Crossing

Name _____

Match up each character in the column on the left to the thing that describes something about him or her in the column on the right.

1. Centipede

2. James

3. Aunt Sponge and Aunt Spiker

4. Spider

5. Old-Green-Grasshopper

6. Earthworm

7. Silkworm

8. Mr. and Mrs. Trotter

9. Ladybug

10. Glow-worm

A. Became the torch for the Statue of Liberty

B. Lived in Central Park inside the peach stone

C. Used as bait for the sea gulls

D. Bit through the strings that were tied to the sea gulls.

E. Squashed flat by the rolling peach

F. Made beds for everyone

G. Married the head of the Fire Department

H. Helped Miss Spider spin string to tie to the sea gulls

I. Got eaten up by an angry rhinoceros

J. Played music with his back leg and wing

What Happens Next?

Name _____

Tell what happened next after each of these sentences.

"And you—Centipede!" James shouted. "Hop downstairs and get that Silkworm to work at once! Tell him to spin as he's never spun before! Our lives depend upon it! And the same applies to you, Miss Spider! Hurry on down! Start spinning!"

_____

_____

"Just _wait_ till I get my hands on him," Aunt Spiker said, waving her cane. "He'll never want to stay out all night again by the time _I've_ finished with him. Good gracious me! What's that awful noise?"

_____

_____

Then he noticed that there was a small door cut into the face of the peach stone. He gave a push. It swung open. He crawled through it, and before he had time to glance up and see where he was, he heard a voice saying, "_Look_ who's here!" And another one said, "We've been _waiting_ for you!"

_____

_____

"But what tremendous tall buildings!" exclaimed the Ladybug. "I've never seen any-thing like them before in England. Which town do you think it is?"

_____

_____

James tiptoed a little closer to the tree. The aunts were not talking now. They were just standing there, staring at the peach. There was not a sound anywhere, not even a breath of wind, and overhead the sun blazed down upon them out of a deep blue sky.

_____

_____

Read All About It

Name _____

Write a newspaper article about your favorite part of *James and the Giant Peach.* Then draw a picture to go along with the story.

The Daily Tribune

What Might Happen If...

As students read chapters from *The Whipping Boy*, ask them to note down events that happened in the book but no longer occur in today's time. For example, the book centered on a royal family, but most countries are no longer ruled by royalty. Another example is the fact that this royal family had a whipping boy who withstood the punishments meant for a prince; families today no longer tolerate this type of cruel behavior.

Discuss the findings of the class each day and compare and contrast their notes. Ask students to choose one event from the book and write about it in detail. Each student should fold a sheet of paper in half. Title one half of the paper "Then," and the other half "Now." Under "Then," tell students to write about the event they have chosen to describe; under "Now," have students write about how the event would be handled nowadays.

Bind the papers together to create a class book. Volunteers may design a cover page for it. Place it on a bookshelf for students to read during free time.

The Whipping Boy Crossword

Name

Solve this puzzle by filling in the words from the story of *The Whipping Boy*.

Across

2. A carefree adventure
3. The king sent these men to find his son
5. Cutwater and Hold-Your-Nose Billy
7. A purebred animal or well-bred person
8. Jemmy's word for scavenging
11. A pier where ships load and unload their goods
12. Where Prince Horace lived
13. Prince Horace's nickname

Down

1. What the king offered to anyone who found the whipping boy
3. Jemmy and the prince ran in these underground tunnels
4. A cluster of leaves and trees
6. The opposite of knowledge
9. Oh, my goodness!
10. Prickly plants or bushes

Name _____

Alex just finished writing a book report about *The Whipping Boy*. Unfortunately, there are a number of mistakes in the report. Read the report. Then fix the grammar, spelling, punctuation, and any factual errors that have been made.

The whipping Boy is about an orfan named jemmy who becomes frends with a prince. After Jemmy serves as the whiping boy for the prince who is called Prince Brat the two boys runned away together. There adventures include tricking some villins and being chased thru dark sewers.

I recomend The Whipping Boy because its an exciting book thats fun to read.

Parts of Speech

Name
_____

Identify the different parts of speech in these sentences from *The Whipping Boy*. Circle each verb, draw a rectangle around each noun, and underline each adjective or adverb.

1. The prince's eyes widened and his face blanched white.

2. The king's men were clearly looking for the vanished prince, but when a bear poked its head out the door window, the soldiers stepped back and quickly waved the coach on.

3. Jemmy led the way through a tarred forest of wharf pilings and over a derelict river barge.

4. The whipping boy learned to read, write, and do sums.

5. Cutwater wiped his thin, greasy lips with the back of his hand.

6. "I swear there are not two more ignorant, cloven-footed blockheads in the land."

7. It felt friendly and trusting.

8. He waved a bamboo pole with long paper streamers fluttering from the tip.

9. Prince Brat sat sullenly on a pile of moldy bed straw.

10. Retreating toward the golden doors, the prince beside him, Jemmy felt a sparkle rise in his eyes.

It's Poetry to Me

Read some different forms of poetry to the class. Ask if any students have favorite poems that they would like to share with the class.

Write "poetry" in the center of the chalkboard or on a large sheet of paper. Then brainstorm about the word "poetry" with the class. Write down all student comments around the word. Discuss the comments.

Explain to students that poems do not have to rhyme; there are forms of poetry such as free verse, haiku, and cinquain. Forms that must rhyme include couplets, quatrains, clerihews, and limericks. Some definitions:

free verse—may or may not rhyme; has no particular form; writer is free to say whatever he or she wishes

haiku—no rhyme, but must contain three lines and seventeen syllables (five in the first line, seven in the second, and five in the last)

cinquain—no rhyme, but must conform to five lines: the first is a one word title, the second is two words describing the title, the third is three words showing action about the title, the fourth is four words expressing a feeling about the title, and the fifth is a one-word synonym for the title

couplet—pairs of lines that usually rhyme

quatrains—four lines with the rhyming pattern AABB

clerihew—a short poem about a famous person whose name is the first line of the poem and follows a rhyming pattern of AABB

Ask students to choose a form of poetry they would like to try. Then have them write poems in the selected forms about an event or a feeling they get from *The Whipping Boy*. When they are finished, encourage students to share their poems with the class, explaining in which forms they wrote, and how they got their ideas for the poems.

War: What It Means

Ask students for their comments on the subject of war. Discuss different aspects of war, such as destruction of property, loss of life, separated families, starvation, the military, and political aftereffects.

Encourage students to bring in news clippings that focus on the subject of war. These could be articles on prior wars, or they could be about recent uprisings and conflicts. Try to show photographs of people who are caught in a fighting zone and elicit feelings from students about how these people might feel and think about their situations.

Trace a recent struggle to its roots to help students understand how conflicts arise and why world leaders cannot always settle matters with diplomacy. Follow the events of the conflict until its outbreak into open hostility and violence.

Discuss what warfare does to people living in a war zone: family members are taken to serve as soldiers in the war, military personnel as well as civilians are hurt and killed or forced to move away, land and animals suffer, food is sometimes depleted to the point that there is starvation, and the struggle sometimes lasts for years.

Ask students if they can think of any advantages to a war. Some suggestions are: sometimes there is an increase in jobs due to production of war products (planes, ships, weaponry, clothing); sometimes a government that has hurt its people is overthrown and a better one takes its place; the standard of living is sometimes higher after a war due to rebuilding and goal-setting; sometimes there is a greater understanding about a people than there was beforehand; and various countries may unite to try and support and take in people from a war-ravaged country.

Gather students in a circle and ask if anybody has any comments to make on the advantages and disadvantages of war. Keep going around the circle until everyone has had a chance to say what he or she wishes or respond to comments made by others.

Paper Cranes

MATERIALS:

one 6" square of paper per crane

DIRECTIONS:

1. Fold the paper in half horizontally. Fold both layers on the dotted lines, as shown.
2. Reverse fold the top layer of the left section. Fold both layers of the left section down the center, as shown.
3. Pull the center open at the places and in the directions indicated in the diagram to make a square, as shown.
4. Fold the top layer of the right and left sides in, as shown. Fold both layers of the top of the square down, as shown.
5. Your model should look like this.
6. Unfold the right and left sides you folded inward in step 4. Pull the bottom point of the top layer up, as shown in figure 6A. The point should now be in the position indicated in figure 6B. Fold down the sides to the back.
7. Turn your model over and repeat step 6.
8. Your model should now look like this.
9. Fold along the dotted lines as indicated on the top layer only (figure 9A). Turn the model over and repeat this step for the other layer (figure 9B).
10. Reverse fold the tail and neck sections inside out, as shown.
11. Reverse fold the top part of the neck section to make the head, as shown.
12. Bend the two remaining sections to form the wings, as shown.

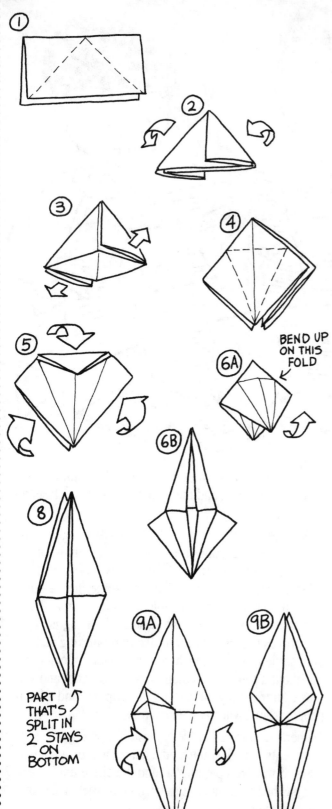

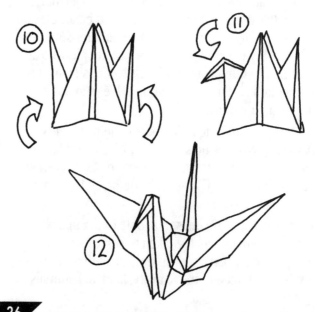

World War II Documentary

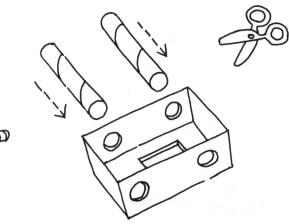

Split the class into research groups. Assign each group a different aspect of World War II: the cause of the original conflict; efforts to settle the conflict and who made the first move toward war; weaponry used and tactics employed; secondary countries who got drawn into the fighting; effects on each country that participated in the war; political outcome for the countries involved.

Allow plenty of time for students to research books, news and magazine articles, and television documentaries about the war. Encourage students to share interesting facts with the class as they come across them.

When notes have been completed and students are familiar with the causes and effects of the war, ask groups to illustrate their findings in filmstrip form. Give the groups construction paper and markers. Demonstrate how to make strips of paper and join them together at the ends to form one long 5" wide strip.

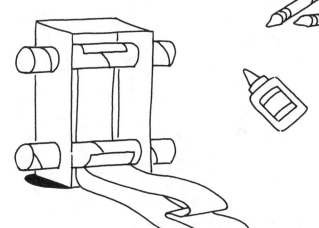

Then have groups illustrate their notes, highlighting events and people from their research. Draw a line about every 7″ to separate different frames or scenes. Ask each group to write a few sentences on each frame so viewers will understand the pictures better. When all the groups have finished, attach the strips together in chronological order.

Cut a 5" x 7" window from the bottom of a shoe box. Stand the box on a short end and cut two holes opposite each other in the long sides of the box, one pair toward the top and one pair toward the bottom. Fit a paper towel roll in each pair of holes so it extends out each side.

Glue the top of the first frame to the top roll and the bottom of the last frame to the bottom roll. Wind the bottom roll so the filmstrip wraps itself around it. To view the filmstrip, roll the top and bottom rollers at the same time. Remember to rewind when the presentation is done!

More or Less

Name _____

Fill in each problem below with **<** or **>**.

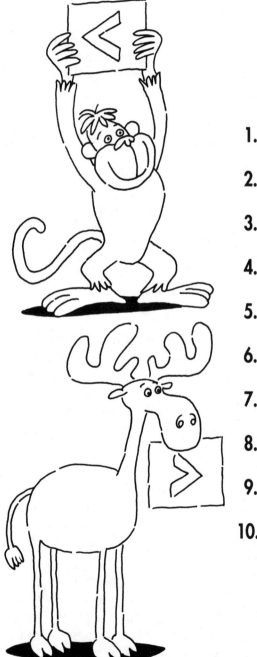

1. 1,642 _____ 1,123

2. 15,654 _____ 18,976

3. 6,467 _____ 7,433

4. 9,211 _____ 9,233

5. 27,700 _____ 29,700

6. 42,611 _____ 47,905

7. 8,144 _____ 12,973

8. 32,067 _____ 32,068

9. 14,896 _____ 25,956

10. 56,874 _____ 58,674

Sadako's Pronouns

Name _____

Pronouns are words that substitute for nouns. Circle the pronouns in the sentences below from *Sadako and the Thousand Paper Cranes*.

1. She cupped the insect in her hands and carefully set it free outside.

2. The next morning the Sasaki family joined crowds of people as they visited their shrines.

3. "You tricked me!" he said with a grin. "But I'll do it anyhow."

4. "I just know," he said.

5. He wanted to sleep as long as possible, but like most fourteen-year-old boys, he also loved to eat.

6. Maybe, she dreamed, I will be the best runner in the whole school.

7. As if he knew what was in Sadako's mind, her father said gruffly, "There now, don't worry. After a good night's rest you'll feel fine."

8. She barely heard him say, "It's time to rest. You can make more birds tomorrow."

On a separate piece of paper, try to rewrite these sentences using nouns whenever possible.

First-Person Interview

When assigning a chapter or a portion of the book to the class, ask each student to write down some questions about Karana's adventures on the island. For example, students may wonder after reading Chapter 7 what Karana was thinking as she plunged into the sea trying to reach her brother, who was still on the shore.

After one or two chapters, ask a volunteer to portray a character of his or her choosing. Have the volunteer come to the front of the room to be interviewed while the rest of the class acts as reporters. Students may ask any questions relevant to the story, and the volunteer must try to answer them as the chosen character might have.

Some character suggestions are: Chief Chowig as he watched the Aleut ship coming closer; Captain Orlov as he formulated his plan to leave the island without any payment to the tribe; Ramo when he saw the ship leaving the island without him; Ulape as Karana jumped from the ship into the sea; Karana realizing she is alone on the island and the boat is not coming back; the people on the ship who discovered Karana alone on the island; and Karana as she tries to adjust to life away from the island.

Tape the interviews to be played back later during student's free time.

Karana's Island

Name _____

Based upon information from *Island of the Blue Dolphins,* draw a map that shows some or all of the things listed below.

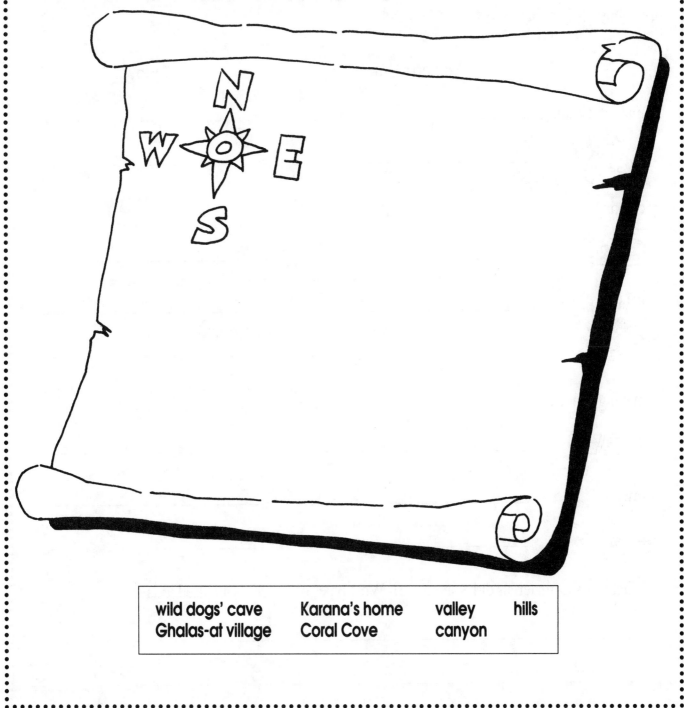

| wild dogs' cave | Karana's home | valley | hills |
| Ghalas-at village | Coral Cove | canyon | |

Chores Then and Now

Name _____

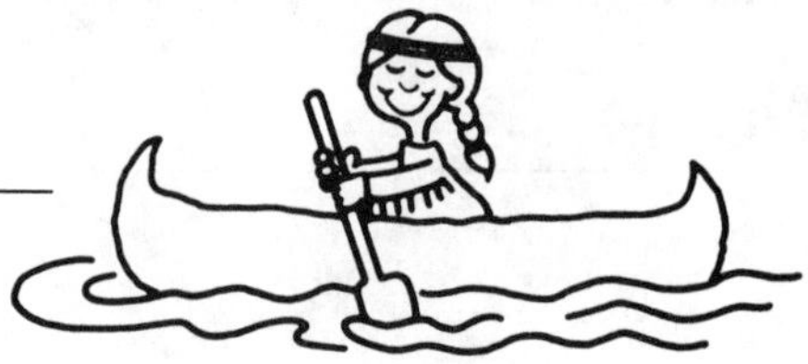

Karana and her people had to perform a number of tasks that are done by machines today. Write descriptions of how Karana did the things listed below. Then write how each job is done today.

	Karana's time	Today
making clothing 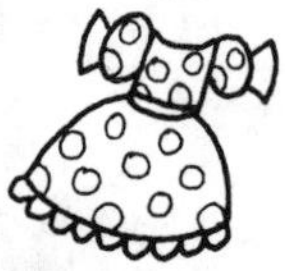	_____ _____	_____ _____
cooking 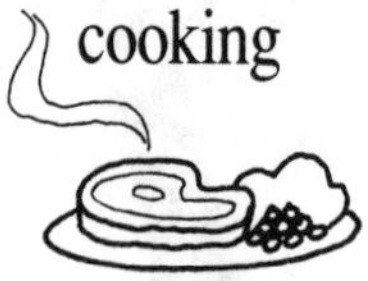	_____ _____	_____ _____
fishing 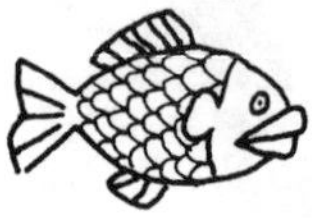	_____ _____	_____ _____
making canoes 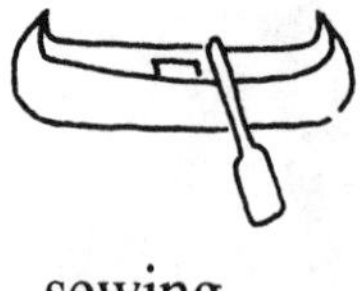	_____ _____	_____ _____
sewing 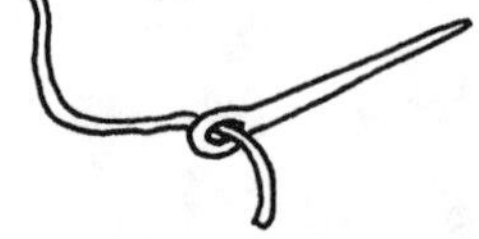	_____ _____	_____ _____

What types of materials did Karana use? What types of materials are used today?

_____

_____

Useful Inventions

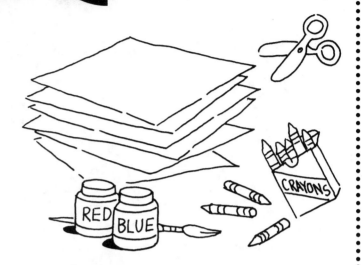

MATERIALS:

clean junk
masking tape
glue
construction paper
scissors
crayons or markers
paint and paintbrushes

DIRECTIONS:

1. Ask each student to think up an invention that would have been useful on the island. Students may wish to make objects that would have been used as defense from the wild dogs, for catching fish, as shelter for Karana, and as a keeping place for food so the dogs could not get at it.

2. Distribute the junk on the tables or floor area. Clean junk may include such items as cardboard containers, sheets of wrapping paper, ribbon, bows, fabric scraps, boxes, handles, old toys, wheels, plastic eating utensils, string, and so on. Have plenty of extra construction paper, masking tape, and glue on hand.

3. Tell students to use the junk to create something that would have helped Karana on the island. Encourage students to try to have at least one moving part on each invention.

4. When students have completed their inventions, they may share them with the rest of the class. Encourage the children to tell how they got their ideas, how they created their inventions, and the purpose of the invention. Then display the inventions around the room for all to see and try.

43

Divide the class into groups to research different parts of the world and the animals that live there. Tell students to gather other information about their world sections, too. Ask them to discuss climate, food sources, terrain (jungle, forest, water, ground), and the characteristics of the animals.

Tell students to connect all this information with the animals to discover how an animal's surroundings affect its behavior, eating patterns, waking hours, body characteristics (small/big, fur/skin, food intake, etc.).

Give each group different-colored paper and tell them to draw small pictures of the types of animals found in their sections of the world. Ask students to pin their animals in the appropriate locations on a world map. Compare and contrast the different places animals can be found and the climates in which they flourish.

When I Am Old Book

MATERIALS:

- crayons or markers
- 12" x 18" construction paper
- scissors
- oaktag
- wrapping paper or bulletin board paper
- glue
- needle and thread
- colored masking tape

DIRECTIONS:

1. When students are finished reading *How Does it Feel to Be Old?*, ask them to imagine what they will look like when they are old themselves. Show the students pictures of elderly people, encouraging them to describe their faces and movements.

2. Distribute a sheet of 12″ x 18″ construction paper to each student. Show them how to fold their papers into fourths. Ask them to draw, or create with paper and glue, self-portraits of themselves now, and how they think they will look when they are 40 years old, and again at 80 years old. In one of the boxes, ask students to write paragraphs about what they think they will be doing when they are 40 years old and 80 years old. Be sure to point out that many elderly people are very energetic and productive, with varied interests and hobbies. Ask students to describe elderly people they know who lead interesting and challenging lives.

3. To make a cover for the book, cut two pieces of oaktag 1" larger than the construction paper pages. Lay them down on an even larger sheet of wrapping paper or bulletin board paper, about 3" bigger than the oaktag sheets lying side by side.

4. Leave 1" between the two sheets of oaktag, then glue them onto the center of the paper.

5. Fold in the corners of the paper, then along the sides, and glue down onto the oaktag. Place the pages inside the cover, centered between them.

6. With needle and thread, stitch up the center of the book, binding the pages into the cover. Wrap masking tape over it to hide the stitches.

7. Close the book and press down to make a crease in the tape. Share the book with the class. Encourage the students to make comments about their drawings and ask questions about others. Leave the books on a bookshelf for viewing during free time, or share them with other classes.

When You Were Younger

Tell the class that they will be interviewing older people they know about their childhoods. Ask the students to think up questions that would elicit information from their subjects about what the world was like when they were younger. Some suggested questions are:

> How many people lived in your house/apartment when you were a child? Who were they?
>
> What was your neighborhood/surrounding area like?
>
> What did you do for fun?
>
> Describe your school and tell which subjects were your favorites.
>
> Who was your favorite person when you were a child and why?
>
> Did you have television or radio? If so, what was your favorite program?
>
> What were your favorite books?

Tell students they may take notes, tape record, take pictures, or video-tape their interviews as long as they first obtain permission from their subjects. Encourage students to broaden their questioning if particular topics interest them about their subjects. If possible, ask students to get old photographs that show each subject's neighborhood, favorite toy, or clothing worn long ago.

When an interview is complete, instruct the students to write it down properly in a question-and-answer format. Students may play their tape recordings or show pictures or videotapes as they share their interviews with the class.

46

Way Back When

Name _____

When your grandparents and great-grandparents were young, everything cost much less than it does today. Look at the prices for the items below. In the blank spaces under the "Now" column, write what you think these things cost today. Then figure out the percentage each item has increased.

	Then	Now	Percent Increase
Movie ticket	10¢	_____	_____
Candy bar	5¢	_____	_____
Soda	5¢	_____	_____
Car	$100	_____	_____
House	$10,000	_____	_____
Hardcover book	50¢	_____	_____
Gallon of milk	10¢	_____	_____
Bicycle	$5	_____	_____

Graph It Up!

HOW DOES IT FEEL TO BE OLD?
by Norma Farber

Name ______________________________

Use the graph below to chart the ages of your parents, siblings, grandparents, aunts, uncles, and cousins. Fill in each person's name, beginning with the oldest person in your family and continuing down to the youngest. Then find the year he or she was born in the columns on the right and fill in the appropriate box. (Fill in the box to the right for anyone born in a year ending with "0" or "5.")

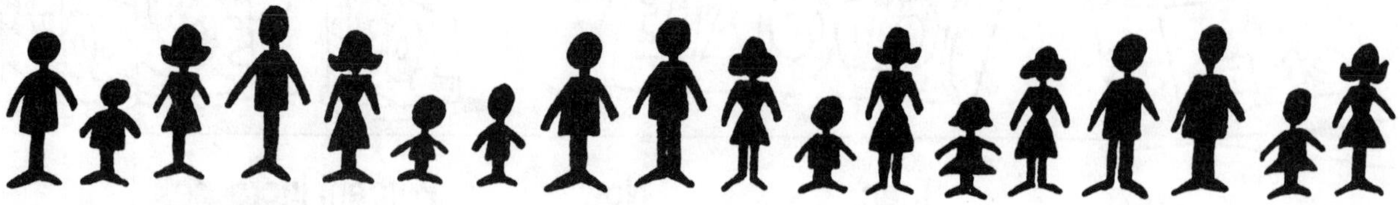

NAMES	19__	1925	1930	1935	1940	1945	1950	1955	1960	1965	1970	1975	1980	1985	1990	1995	2000

My Autobiography

Tell the students they will be writing autobiographies. Ask them if they can define what the word means. If necessary, explain that it is a life history of a particular person written by himself or herself.

Ask the class to make notes on their childhoods: who influenced them, their families, favorite toys and foods, their hopes, and other subjects they wish to add. Then ask the students to write their predictions on what they think they will be doing 40 years from now, and what the world will be like. Or, if students prefer, they may wish to write about parts of their lives today.

Suggested topics to focus on are: government, the environment, violence, futuristic travel, futuristic inventions, and housing. When writing their autobiographies, students should make each topic a new chapter, separated by a chapter page.

Bind the chapters together and add a sturdy front and back cover. Ask the students to design a cover and title for their books. Leave them on the bookshelf for all to read and enjoy.

49

Opposites Attract

Name

An **antonym** is a word that has the opposite meaning of another word. Fill in the antonyms of the words below to complete the crossword puzzle.

Across

2. Shorter
3. Slow
7. Forget
9. Cowardly
10. Mean
12. Praise
16. Old
17. Late
18. Easy
19. Go

Down

1. Wobbly
2. Free
4. **Smaller**
5. Smooth
6. End
8. Cold
9. After
11. Shy
13. Hating
14. Clear
15. Stretch

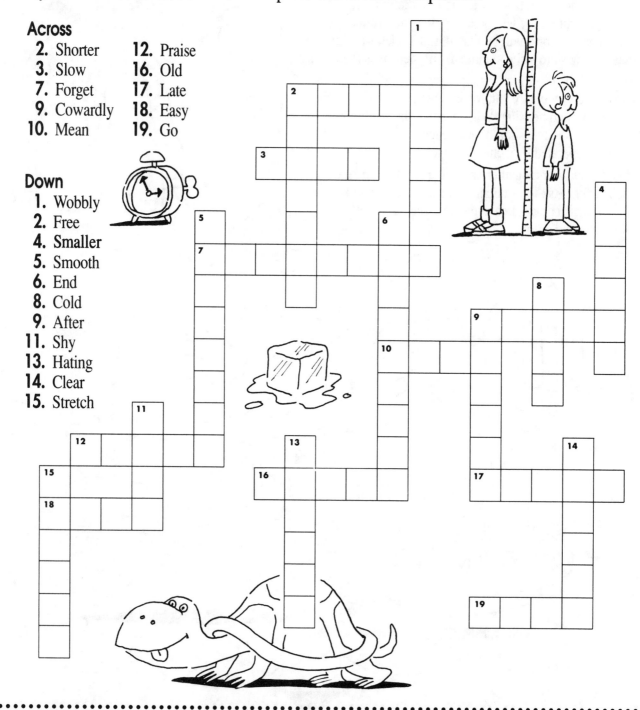

The Real-Life Pretend Toys

Ask students to think of their favorite toys or hobbies coming to life. Discuss what it might be like to have a stamp collection or a favorite character from a book share a few days as a real object that can talk, think, feel, and move.

Ask the class what they think might happen if their wishes came true and a favorite toy did become real. How might the toy cope with the real world? How might the students feel realizing something that was fake is now a living, breathing thing?

Tell the class they will be making storybooks about toys that come to life using text and illustrations. Ask the students to create a story based on one of their possessions that comes to life. Some suggested chapter headings are: the toy before it becomes alive; why and how it becomes real; the first reactions of the student and the toy to the event; adventure(s) they have together; whether or not the toy stays real or goes back to its original form, and why and how.

The students may decide whether they wish to bind their stories into one big class book or make individual books. When the covers and titles are finished, make an appointment with the younger-grade teachers to read the stories to their classes.

Native American Masks

MATERIALS:

newspaper
masking tape
flour and water paste
paints and paintbrushes
collage materials
shellac

DIRECTIONS:

1. Show the students books about Native American masks. Discuss the differences the class sees among the masks. Ask them to compare and contrast masks. Why do students think certain masks show a particular emotion, and why are the masks shaped differently? Then encourage them to research their answers.

2. Demonstrate to students how to form a shape with sheets of newspaper. Ball the sheets together until the ball is about 6" deep. Then begin to change the shape into the mask by wrapping newspaper nearer one end than the other and by squaring off or rounding out edges. Use masking tape sparingly. Press the mask shape into a flat surface so the back becomes flat.

3. Make a paste of flour and water. Place two cups of flour in a bowl, then add water and stir. Keep adding water gradually until the paste feels thick but pourable.

4. Rip strips of newspaper. Dunk them into the paste, then spread them in a layer over the mask shape. Make sure the layer is as smooth as possible. When adding new layers, try to face the print on the paper a different way so the layers will be easier to count.

5. After the second layer, begin making features for the mask. Wad balls of newspaper in the desired shape for a nose, forehead, eyes, or other decoration and tape in place. Then add new layers of newspaper stripping.

6. When the features are done and the mask is dry, paint it. When the paint dries, add a coat of shellac. Add any collage materials necessary to make the mask look like it has hair, facial decorations, jewelry, and other Native American accessories. Encourage the students to share their masks and the process by which they made them with the class. Put the masks on display out in a showcase for the whole school to see and discuss.

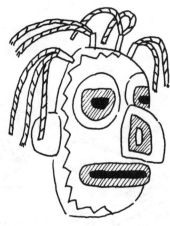

Hidden Diaries

Ask the class who is the teller (narrator) of the story in *The Indian in the Cupboard*. How would the story be different if it was told from the point of view of Boone, Little Bear, Adiel, or Patrick?

Tell the students that they will each be writing a diary from the perspective of a character in the story. Give them a chapter to read and ask students to choose a character in the chapter. They will then describe the events in the chapter using the language of their chosen character.

Encourage the class to include how they think the character felt about a particular event, what they might have been thinking, explanations for various behavior, and their opinion of the other characters. For example, in Chapter 15, when the Indian is asked to go under the floorboards to retrieve the key to the cupboard and gets chased by Gillon's rat, what do students think he was saying to himself and feeling?

Ask students if they would like to share their diaries with the class. After a student has read his or her diary, the others may guess which character is being portrayed. Elicit from students why they chose a particular character and why they feel the character would take the attitude the student gave him or her.

Make Your Own Flip Book

MATERIALS:

3" x 5" index cards
markers
stapler

DIRECTIONS:

1. Ask the class to share their favorite scenes from *The Indian in the Cupboard*. Tell them that they will be making flip books about these scenes.

2. Distribute index cards and markers to the students. Explain that to make a flip book, one must break an action scene into steps. For example, when Omri saves the Indian from the rat under the floorboards, three cards may be drawn showing Omri placing the Indian down in the floor, three may be drawn with Omri looking in, three may be drawn showing the Indian coming back holding the key, and the last three may show Omri taking the Indian out while the rat looks on.

3. When the scenes have been broken down and drawn, test the book by placing the cards in a pile with the first scene on top. Hold the left side and flip the book on the right side. The pages, when flipped, should show an animated drawing of the student's favorite scene.

4. If enough cards have been drawn to show a smooth action, add a cover sheet to the top of the pile and staple it to the book.

5. Encourage students to share their flip books, with the class trying to guess which scene it is.

Fry Bread

Make this Native American recipe with the class after completing *The Indian in the Cupboard*.

MATERIALS:

5 cups flour
2 1/2 tablespoons powdered milk
1 1/4 teaspoons salt
1 1/4 teaspoons baking powder
2 cups warm water
1 1/4 cups vegetable oil
butter, honey, and/or cinnamon
large mixing bowl
sifter
fork
towel
frying pan
spatula

Yields: 1 dozen loaves

DIRECTIONS:

1. Ask several students to sift the flour, salt, powdered milk, and baking powder together in a large bowl.
2. Have another student slowly add the warm water to the mixture while a classmate stirs with a fork. Continue stirring until the mixture becomes dough-like.
3. Tell two students to knead the dough for several minutes until it becomes elastic.
4. Cover the dough with a towel for 10-15 minutes and let it rise.
5. Have students take pieces of the dough and flatten them to make loaves approximately 5" in diameter.
6. Place the vegetable oil in a frying pan and heat over medium heat. When the oil is hot enough, place one of the dough loaves in the pan. (Caution students to stay away from the pan in case the oil splatters.)
7. Fry the bread until it is golden brown on both sides. Serve with butter, honey, and/or cinnamon if desired.

Pioneer Days

Brainstorm with the class on the topic of pioneer days. Encourage students to call out comments on the subject and write them on a chalkboard or a large sheet of paper.

Tell the students to find a comment mentioned during brainstorming in which they are interested. Have them link up with classmates who are also interested in the same topic.

When all the students have joined a group, ask them to research their topics. They may use books, films, television, newspapers and magazines, and interviews to help them discover facts about their topics.

As the groups are nearing the end of their research, tell them that they will be presenting their information to the class. Ask them to create ideas on how they will conduct their presentations. They may make a video, take pictures of a re-enactment, lecture, make up an advertising campaign, visit a museum or restoration village then talk about what they learned, make up a song that illustrates an event or way of life among pioneers, or sew an outfit for a boy and girl that was worn in those days.

Arrange the work on display around the room and invite other classes in to view the ''Pioneer Museum.''

The People Could Fly Mural

MATERIALS:

    newspapers
    mural paper
    pencils
    paints and paintbrushes
    markers
    tissue paper, ribbon, fabric, beads

DIRECTIONS:

1. Create a mural for a school hallway based on the folktales from *The People Could Fly*. Begin by laying out newspapers on the floor of the classroom.

2. Lay a large piece (or pieces) of mural paper on top of the newspapers. Ask each student to choose one of the tales or characters from the book to depict on the mural.

3. Have students sketch out their drawings in pencil. Encourage the children to work together to create small scenes or vignettes.

4. Provide students with paints and markers to use to color in the mural.

5. Give the children other decorating materials, such as tissue paper, ribbon, fabric, and beads to use to complete the mural.

6. Make a banner for the mural that says, "The People Could Fly." Hang the mural and banner in a prominent place for all to see.

Slavery Discussions

Have the students bring chairs into a tight circle, leaving no one out. Open the discussion with the word "slavery." Go around the circle asking if each student has something he or she would like to say about the topic. Encourage students to speak, but do not push a child to talk if he or she does not wish to.

After the first round, tell the students they may get another chance to speak on the topic or respond to what another student has said. Continue going around the circle until it seems all students have spoken if they wanted.

After the discussion, distribute poster paper and markers. Ask students to create posters as abolitionists might have before slavery was abolished.

Display the posters and ask each student to explain his or hers to the class. Place the posters in a school hallway for all to observe.

Class Folktales

MATERIALS:

construction paper
crayons or markers
stapler

DIRECTIONS:

1. Share with the class various folktales from different cultures. Discuss the definition of a folktale (a story having legendary or mythical elements, made up and handed down orally through generations). Ask if students know any folktales from their own culture, perhaps told by a grandparent or other family member.

2. Ask students to create their own folktales. The stories may be about a person or place, an object, an animal, or how something came to be the way it is (i.e., the sun, stars). Have students draft their folktales before they begin writing the text on construction paper.

3. Add a front and back cover and bind the covers and pages by stapling down the left side. These books may be placed on the bookshelf, in the school library, or loaned out to other classes.

Imaginary Interviews

Name _____

What was your favorite tale in *The People Could Fly*? Do you wish you could have read more about the characters in this tale?

Imagine that you could interview one of the characters from your favorite tale. What questions would you ask him or her? What do you think this character would say to you? Write your questions and imaginary answers below. (Use another piece of paper if necessary.) When you are finished, share your interview with the rest of the class.

Q _____   A _____

_____

_____

Q _____   A _____

_____

_____

Q _____   A _____

_____

_____

Q _____   A _____

_____

_____

Character Search

Name

Try to find the names of the characters from *The People Could Fly* that are hidden below. Use the names in the box to help you. The names may be written forward, backward, up, down, or diagonally.

```
A U B R U H D E E R C B A L W A
U J A S N I K N A R R M I D I J
N H O J T H G I E E L T T I L O
T A A H R I A H L W T N H D E H
F N Y R N A R E U L E A W O T I
I H B B T D U Q E H I Y E L I W
S O A N E N E D E M A U H N B C
H J B P A K A C E Q K U P I B O
H A R M A U T H O C F I E P A N
O P A J G I E U A N T O N P R Q
R A T H L N Q J Q U Q H O A C U
S P T B R U H F O X H U R T O A
E E H A I R Y M A N E N E S D F
R W R O T A G I L L A H U R B I
```

Papa John	Jake	Wiley	Hairy Man
John de Conquer	Little Eight John	Jack	Mr. Rankins
Nehemiah	Doc Rabbit	Bruh Fox	Tar Baby
Bruh Alligator	Bruh Deer	Nephew	Aunt Fish-Horse
Anton	Little Daughter		

Can you find two other characters whose names are not in the box?

Monster Animal Costumes

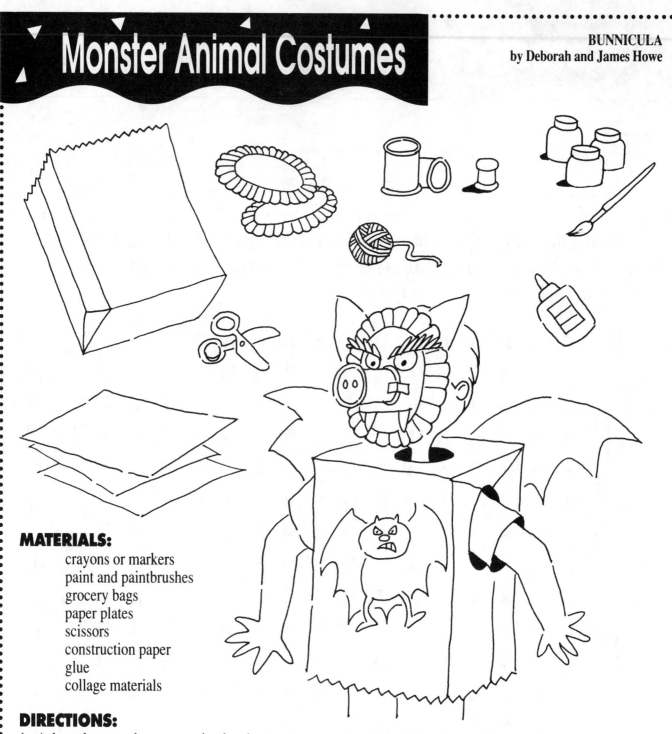

MATERIALS:

crayons or markers
paint and paintbrushes
grocery bags
paper plates
scissors
construction paper
glue
collage materials

DIRECTIONS:

1. Ask students to choose an animal and a monster to combine and name. Encourage them to share their creature combinations with the class. Ask each child how he or she thought of the name and personality of the creature. Encourage the students to create other features, such as favorite foods, favorite activities, dislikes, home, and a unique talent or activity.

2. Tell students that they will be making costumes and/or masks that will bring their creatures to life. To make a body, each student may cut a hole in the bottom of a grocery bag large enough for his or her head to fit through. Then tell each student to cut slits up the sides of the bag to make armholes.

3. Give students paints and crayons or markers to use to decorate their bags.

4. To make masks, students can cut eye holes from paper plates, then draw or glue on collage materials that will enhance their creatures.

5. If desired, let students make leggings or arm coverings for their costumes out of construction paper.

6. When the costumes are finished, let students dress up and show off their creature combinations to the class. Ask them to point out any special decorations or features of the costumes.

Main Ideas

Name

Read each of the paragraphs below. Then circle the sentence that tells what the main idea of each paragraph is.

Every night when the family is sleeping, Chester goes to the bookshelf, selects his midnight reading and curls up on his favorite chair. He especially likes mystery stories and tales of horror and the supernatural. As a result, he has developed a very vivid imagination.

A. Chester likes to read.
B. Chester has a favorite chair.
C. Chester has a vivid imagination.

I don't know if you've ever watched a cat try to decide where to sit, but it involves a lot of circling around, sitting, getting up again, circling some more, thinking about it, lying down, standing up, bathing a paw or tail and...circling! A dog, on the other hand, sits.

A. Dogs are better at making decisions than cats.
B. Cats are lazy.
C. Cats like to take their time in choosing a place to sit.

It was Friday night, and on Friday nights, Toby gets to stay up and read as late as he wants to. So, of course, he needs lots of food to keep up his strength. Good food like cheese crackers, chocolate cupcakes (my very favorite, the kind with cream in the middle, mmmm!), pretzels and peanut butter sandwiches. The last I cannot abide because my mouth always gets stuck.

A. Toby gets to stay up late on Friday nights.
B. Harold loves to have snacks with Toby on Friday nights.
C. Peanut butter sticks in Harold's mouth.

Talking Pets

Name

Do you have a pet or a favorite animal? What do you think this animal would say if it could talk?

Write a story using the voice of your pet or favorite animal. Then draw a picture of the animal to go along with the story.

...AND MY FAVORITE PLACE TO SLEEP IS ON CHARLEY'S PILLOW...

Imaginations Running Wild

Name

In *Bunnicula*, Harold the dog and Chester the cat imagine that Bunnicula is really a vampire rabbit. By the end of their adventure, Harold realizes that Bunnicula is really just an ordinary rabbit—with a little extra magic.

Have you ever let your imagination run wild like Harold and Chester did? Have you ever believed in ghosts or goblins, or some other supernatural powers? Have you ever heard a mysterious noise, or been a part of some eerie adventure? Write about a time when you let your imagination get the better of you!

Panel Discussion

Explain to the class that although people may predict what they think they would do in any given situation, there is no true indicator that their predictions would come true unless the situation really exists for them. It was the same for many men and women during World War II when *Anne Frank: The Diary of a Young Girl* was written.

For example, no one could predict the power and influence one government official, Adolf Hitler, would one day have over Germany. His armies and special branch of police were filled with regular, everyday people. It was only under the specific conditions that Hitler created that these people began to believe in the same things he did. There were also a good number of people who were courageous enough to go against the majority of the country when they hid people from Hitler's army, even though they could have been killed for doing so.

As students read *Anne Frank: The Diary of a Young Girl*, ask them to make notes on behavior that was not usual for certain people in the story and to back up their judgments with evidence from the book. Remind the children that this is a work of nonfiction, and that the people and situations described in the book really existed.

Then choose ten students to sit on a panel and discuss the ethics of following or not following orders. Ask five students to speak on the side of always following orders no matter what, and five students to speak about personal beliefs coming first when it comes to following orders.

Begin with a question, such as, "If you were forced to be a soldier in Hitler's army, would you have helped in his effort to kill millions of people, or would you have rebelled, even if it meant risking your own life?" Other questions for discussion are, "Would you have hidden a Jewish family somewhere in your house during the war? How do you think the families who hid Jewish people in their homes felt? How do you think it felt to be a member of a family in hiding?"

Encourage students in the audience to speak as well, as long as the panel recognizes them and asks them to speak.

Follow-up panel discussions might center on the topic of discrimination and its effects on those who do the discriminating and those who are the brunt of it.

Anne's Room

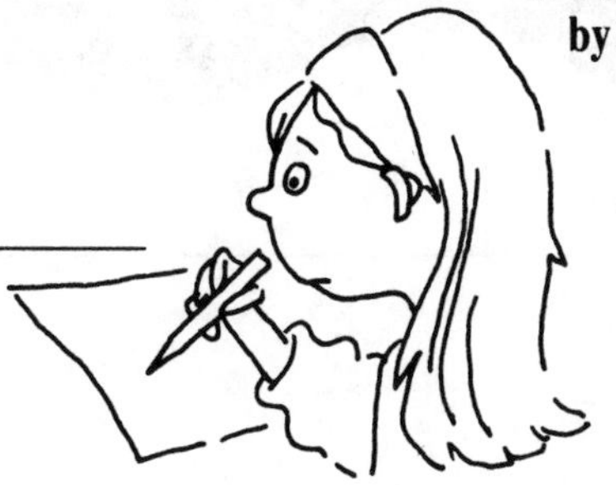

Name _____

What do you think Anne Frank's room looked like? Draw a floor plan below that shows the different rooms, where the furniture was located, and any other important information.

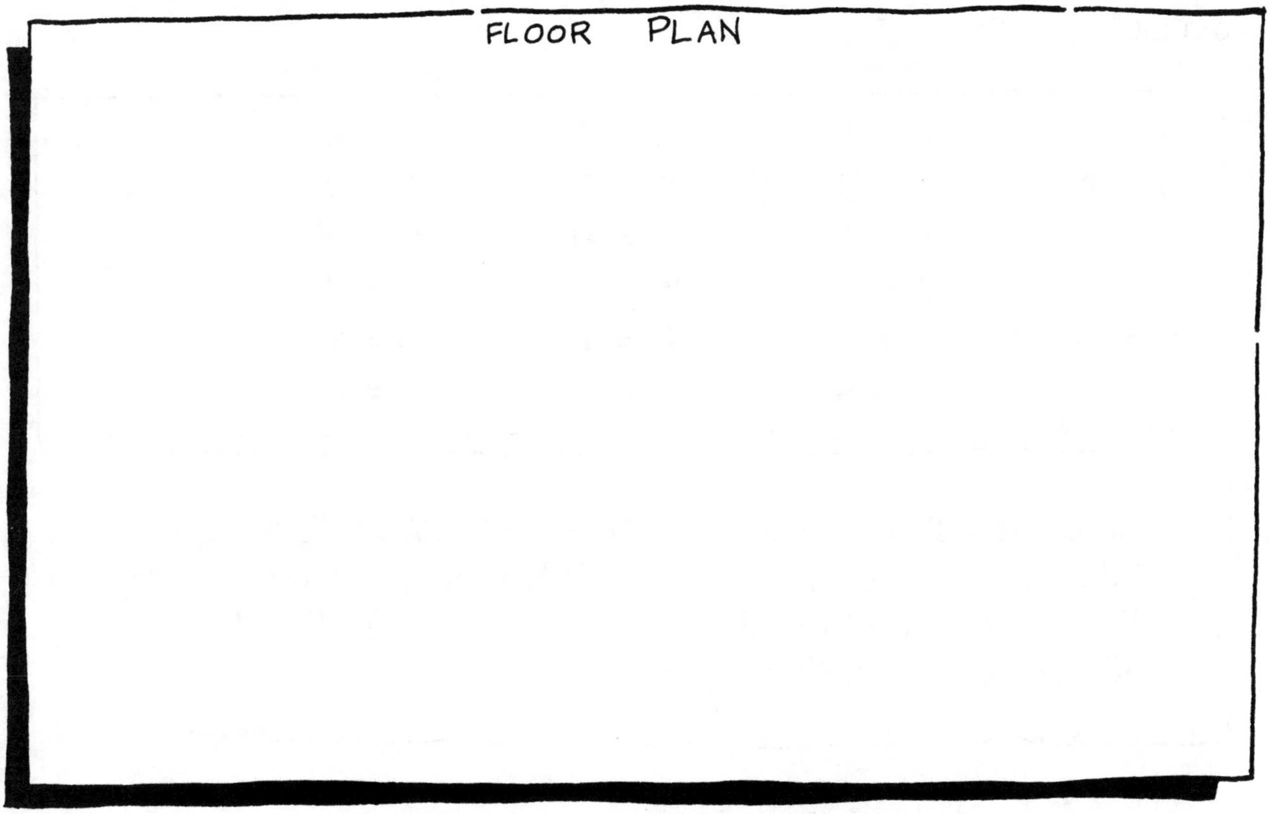

FLOOR   PLAN

How do you think it felt to live in such close quarters with so many people for a long time? _____

_____

_____

How do you think it feels to be in hiding? _____

_____

_____

Break the Code

Name _____

During wartime, people often use secret codes to send important messages. Use this secret code to figure out the diary entry below from *Anne Frank: The Diary of a Young Girl*. Then, on a separate piece of paper, send a friend a message using the code.

A = C	G = I	M = O	S = U	Y = A
B = D	H = J	N = P	T = V	Z = B
C = E	I = K	O = Q	U = W	
D = F	J = L	P = R	V = X	
E = G	K = M	Q = S	W = Y	
F = H	L = N	R = T	X = Z	

K NQXG VCNMKPI VQ RGVGT, DWV K'O CNYCAU CHTCKF QH
DGKPI C PWKUCPEG....JG WUGF VQ VJKPM K YCU WPDGCTCDNG,
CPF K TGVWTPGF VJG EQORNKOGPV; PQY K JCXG EJCPIGF OA
QRKPKQP, JCU JG EJCPIGF JKU VQQ?

_____

_____

_____

_____

_____

_____

Promotional Campaign

Tell the students that they have been hired to be the advertising team who will promote *A Wrinkle in Time*. Ask the students to talk about what happens when a new book, movie, or other product comes out. Encourage them to include such ideas as television and radio commercials, movie previews, posters, magazine and newspaper ads, and talk show interviews.

Divide students into groups based upon the area in which they would like to work: television, radio, or print. Distribute paper, markers, scissors, and a large piece of oaktag to each group. Allow them time to come up with one or two promotional ideas, then illustrate and explain them on a large piece of oaktag.

Call one group at a time to display and explain their campaign. When all the groups have had a chance to pitch their ideas, evaluate with the class how effective the campaign would be if it were real. Ask them to make suggestions and comments on what could have been done differently in their own group to make the campaign a better one.

Display the posters on a classroom wall. As an extension activity, have students come up with campaigns to promote their favorite television shows, movies, parks, or other things of interest.

69

Which One Am I?

When the class has finished reading *A Wrinkle in Time,* tell them that they will be playing a game called Which One Am I? Pick three contestants and one announcer to play the game. Take the three players aside and instruct them that they will be different characters from the book, although they will all tell the audience that they are Meg. Choose one player to actually portray Meg, and ask the two other students to choose their identities for the game.

Have the players sit at the front of the room, facing the audience. Tell the announcer to ask players to state their names (all should say "I am Meg"). Each audience member then gets a chance to ask a yes-or-no question of the players. (The announcer should call on audience members to ask their questions.) Players should answer the questions as their secret characters would.

An audience member may guess at any time who the real Meg is. If he or she guesses correctly, the game is over and a new game may begin, using a different character from the story. If, after ten to fifteen minutes, no one guesses who the real Meg is, the announcer should ask that student to stand before beginning a new game.

Multiplication Mania

Name _____

Meg got upset when IT chanted the multiplication tables. Help Meg out by filling in the missing numbers below.

1. $9 \times \underline{\hspace{0.5cm}} = 54$

2. $10 \times 11 = \underline{\hspace{0.5cm}}$

3. $\underline{\hspace{0.5cm}} \times 8 = 96$

4. $9 \times 9 = \underline{\hspace{0.5cm}}$

5. $7 \times \underline{\hspace{0.5cm}} = 49$

6. $\underline{\hspace{0.5cm}} \times 12 = 72$

7. $\underline{\hspace{0.5cm}} \times 11 = 55$

8. $12 \times 12 = \underline{\hspace{0.5cm}}$

9. $6 \times \underline{\hspace{0.5cm}} = 60$

10. $\underline{\hspace{0.5cm}} \times 8 = 72$

11. $4 \times \underline{\hspace{0.5cm}} = 36$

12. $3 \times 9 = \underline{\hspace{0.5cm}}$

13. $12 \times \underline{\hspace{0.5cm}} = 108$

14. $11 \times 11 = \underline{\hspace{0.5cm}}$

15. $7 \times 9 = \underline{\hspace{0.5cm}}$

Prefix and Suffix Alert

Name

_____

IT wants you to find all the prefixes and suffixes in the sentences below from *A Wrinkle in Time.* Put a circle around the prefixes, and underline all the suffixes. But be careful—IT doesn't take kindly to mistakes!

1. What were her greatest faults? Anger, impatience, stubbornness.

2. His eyes were an oddly bright blue.

3. Or was it a Thing in itself?

4. "What cause have I given you for distrust?" The thin lips curled slightly.

5. There was an air of such ineffable peace and joy all around her that her heart's wild thumping slowed.

6. Aunt Beast stood quietly against the assault.

7. "How extraordinary! I could almost see the atoms rearranging!"

8. It seemed unsubstantial, as though one might almost be able to walk through it.

9. The globe became hazy, cloudy, then shadows began to solidify, to clarify, and they were looking into an untidy kitchen with a sink full of unwashed dishes.

10. "Look at something cheerful, do. I can't bear to have you distressed!"

11. "I've heard that clever people often have subnormal children," Meg had once overheard.

12. "You're like Charles Wallace. Your development has to go at its own pace."

13. But she, in all her weakness and foolishness and baseness and nothingness, was incapable of loving IT.

14. With her inefficient flying tackle she landed on him.

Mapping a Story

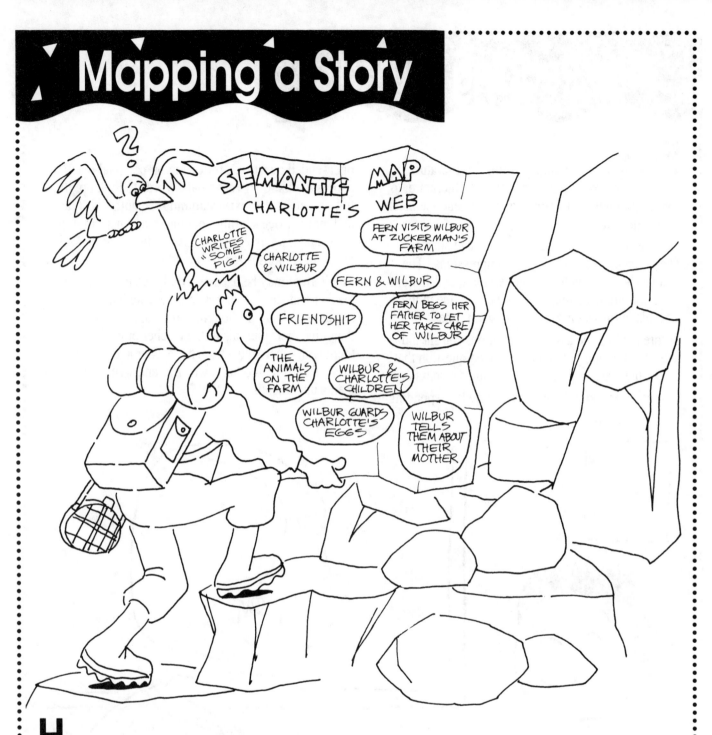

Help students organize the information and main ideas found in a story by creating a semantic map. Write the title of the selected book at the top of the chalkboard. Tell students that they will be making a "map" of the story.

Ask volunteers to name the main idea of the story. Write the idea in the center of the chalkboard. Draw a circle around it.

Then ask volunteers to name some secondary topics that are discussed in the story. Encourage students to think of topics that are both literal and inferential. Write the ideas around the main idea and circle them.

Draw lines to connect the secondary topics to the main idea.

Ask the children to categorize parts of the story under the appropriate topics. After each student suggests a piece of information from the story, have him or her tell where it should be written on the chalkboard.

After the class has mapped out a story together, assign each child a story to map by him- or herself. Then pair students together to go over each other's assignments to see if their partners can think of more information to add to the maps.

The Reading Journal

Some uses of the reading journal, or literature response log, are to record reactions to literature, to connect reading and writing, and to extend the meaning of the text.

Small groups are assigned books to read silently. They then meet to discuss their impressions. The groups should be heterogeneous, small, and student-directed. Students may refer to notes made in their journals during their group discussion time.

Before reading the assigned selection, you should focus the reading with an open-ended question that can be the starting point for the group's discussions.

Responses in journals should be varied: responding to open-ended questions, reflecting on personal reactions, choosing unknown vocabulary words to look up, illustrating part of the text, examining the author's style and motive, free writing, imagining another point of view, and making up questions for discussion. Assign different responses for each reading.

The journal may be used as a dialogue between the teacher and student, or between two students. Students write their thoughts on what they have read, then give their journals to the teacher or exchange them with other students. The teacher and students may react to each other's writings and write their comments underneath.

I Know That! Game

HOW TO PLAY: (for 2 to 4 players)

1. The youngest player goes first. Play continues clockwise.

2. Each player places his or her playing piece on "Start." The first player rolls the die and moves the number of spaces indicated.

3. The player must draw a card from the pile whose color corresponds to the space he or she has landed on. If the question is answered correctly, the player continues play. If the question is answered incorrectly, the player must wait until his or her next turn to try again. Then the next player goes.

4. If a player lands on a colored space and answers that question correctly, he or she receives a token. The first player to collect six tokens (one of each color) wins the game.

MATERIALS:

> crayons or markers
> scissors
> file folder
> glue
> clear contact paper
> construction paper
> die
> large envelope

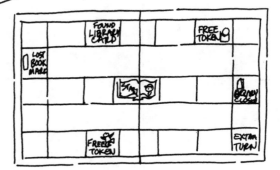

DIRECTIONS:

1. Reproduce the game board once and the game card patterns ten times (pages 76-78). Color and cut out the board.

2. Glue the game board to the inside of a file folder.

3. Color sets of ten game cards different colors. With a black crayon or marker, write the categories of books to be used in the game: mystery, science fiction, comedy, adventure, fables and folktales, biographies. Make sure the game card color matches the color of the space on the board featuring that category.

4. On the back of each card, write a question about a book, character, setting, or plot under the category written on the front of the game card. Some examples of questions:

- What was the name of Laura Ingall's teacher?
- What year did Anne Frank go into hiding?
- How many paper cranes did Sadako make?

5. Laminate the game cards with clear contact paper.

6. Make playing pieces by cutting 1″ squares of different-colored construction paper for each player. Laminate these with clear contact paper.

7. To make tokens, cut out sets of six circles from different-colored construction paper. Make sure each set matches a color used for the game cards.

8. Glue an envelope to the back of the file folder to store game cards, playing pieces, a die, and tokens.

I Know That! Game

I Know That! Game

YOU FINISHED READING A BOOK!
FREE TOKEN

LIBRARY CLOSED!
LOSE A TURN

FINISHED YOUR BOOK REPORT!
EXTRA TURN!

77

I Know That! Game

DIRECTIONS:

1. Reproduce the game card patterns on page 78 several times. Color the patterns and cut them out.

2. Tell students that they will receive one minibook award each time they finish a book not assigned to them in class. In order to get the award, explain to the class that each child must present either a written or an oral report on the book he or she has read.

3. When the report is accepted, write the title of the book and the author's name on the cover.

4. Set a goal for the students. For example, if they get ten awards, they may present them to the teacher for a prize. Some prize suggestions are: a book, extra reading time, extra free time, a new pen, or a journal.

To integrate classroom learning, help students create books based on the time periods depicted in some of the books they have read. Since these original books may be quite complicated in their designs, you may want to have the children work in groups of four to six students each for some of the projects.

For example, students may wish to make medieval-type books after reading *The Whipping Boy*. After each group has written a rough draft of the story, have them sketch out thumbnail illustrations for the cover and interior pages of the book. Help students research and practice calligraphy writing and learn how to draw illuminated lettering. Give each group a 9" x 12" piece of tin to use as a cover for their book. Have students sketch out a picture on the back of the tin. Students will then raise the image from the tin by placing the flat end of a screwdriver (or similar object)

along their sketch lines and hammering the top of the screwdriver. Tell students to be sure to leave room for a calligraphy treatment for the title on the cover as well.

After reading *The Diary of Anne Frank*, students may wish to create their own wartime diaries. Begin by letting students research what life was like in different areas of Europe, Japan, and America during World War II. Have students tie looseleaf pages together and use pencils to evoke the feeling of rationing and having to do without everyday comforts. Ask some students to pretend they are children in hiding, like Anne Frank. Ask others to write their diaries as if they are free people who are observing what is going on in the world. Encourage students to share their books with the rest of the class by placing them in the reading center when they are completed.

Student Book Journals

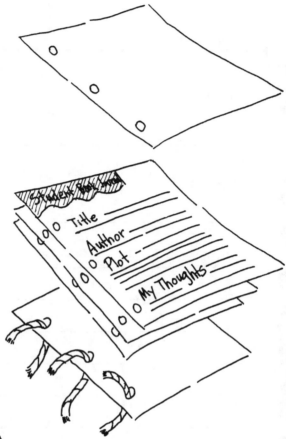

To help students keep records of the books they have read, ask each child to start a book journal. Reproduce the journal form on page 82 twenty times for each child. Have students mount the forms on construction paper and punch holes along the left sides. Students may also wish to use construction paper to make covers for their journals. Tie the pages together with yarn so that pages may be added as needed.

After a child has completed a book, have him or her write about it in the journal. Tell students to include some or all of this information in their writings:

What was the plot of the book?

What did you like or dislike about the book?

Describe the main character and other important characters.

What type of book was it (i.e., mystery, action, nonfiction, etc.)?

How did the book make you feel?

Would you like to see a movie made from this book? Why?

Have students write in their journals as soon as possible after finishing a book so their thoughts are fresh. If desired, the children may also wish to make illustrations to go along with their writings.

Once a month, ask each child to present his or her favorite book of the month to the rest of the class. Have each student give a brief oral report telling about the book and why he or she recommends it.

In the back of each journal, have students make a section entitled "Books I'd Like to Read." When a student hears about a book that he or she thinks would be fun to read, that child should record the title and author in this section of the journal. Students may also enjoy bringing their journals on library trips.

At the end of the year, go through each journal with each student. Ask students to think about the different books they have read during the year, and how these books have changed the way they think about things.

Student Book Journals

Title: _____

_____

Author: _____

_____

Plot: _____

_____

_____

_____

_____

_____

_____

_____

My Thoughts: _____

_____

_____

_____

_____

_____

_____

_____

Class Book Party

BOOKS ARE THE BEST

Have a class party at the end of the year with the theme "Books Are the Best!" Begin by dividing the class into different committees to handle the various party preparations. Suggestions for the committees are: invitations, decorations, food and drinks, entertainment, and budget.

Tell each committee to begin by making a list of the things that need to be done. Explain that making lists, sending invitations, planning entertainment, coming up with a budget, and other party preparations are all different forms of reading and writing. Tell students that it is important to use language to get one's meaning across clearly.

Help students enlist the aid of parents, friends, and other school workers in planning their party. Ask students and guests to come to the party dressed as characters from their favorite books. (Be sure to include this request on the invitations.) If possible, allow students class time in the week before the party to work on their costumes. Tell students to keep their characters a secret so that the other guests can try to guess their identities at the party.

Place books around the classroom on the day of the party. Encourage students and guests to discuss any books they have read, and to share their thoughts about these books with others.

Current Events

Each night, assign different students to watch the news or read the newspaper. Ask each student to find a story that interests him or her and to follow the development of the story for a few days.

Next, ask students to write articles that recap the stories as well as provide insights and make predictions based on the developments.

Help the class create a "Current Events" bulletin board. As the students complete their articles, have them tack them to the bulletin board for all to read. Make sure the articles are dated and contain correct information before adding them to the board. Encourage students to keep their news clippings in a scrapbook to help them remember what happened that year.

Assign one student the job of clearing the board as old stories become less newsworthy and new ones come up. This way the board stays clean and the students stay current.

Guess Who?

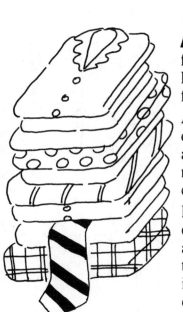

Ask the class to think of their favorite characters from any books they have read during the past year. Discuss who the characters are and why they are favorites.

As a homework assignment, have students dress up as one of the characters mentioned. Give the class about a week to get their costumes together. Costumes need not be elaborate, but should give a sense of who the character is.

Have each student write a short speech to say in front of the class while in costume. Direct students, one at a time, to stand at the front of the room and show off their costumes. They may then say their short speech in the language and voice of the character. See if anyone can guess who they are portraying.

Write to the Author

To help students learn more about writing, ask them to compose letters to their current favorite authors. Encourage students to think of special questions to ask each author, such as:

- When did you first realize you wanted to be a writer?
- What is the best way to learn how to write?
- Where do you get your ideas for your books?
- What is your favorite book that you have written? Why?
- Who is your favorite character from your books? Why?
- What books did you enjoy when you were a child?
- Whom did you admire when you were young? Whom do you admire now?
- Are your books based on personal experiences?
- Have you ever had any other jobs?
- Are any of your friends authors?

Ask students to include information about themselves in their letters, and tell why they enjoy each author's writing. If possible, read the book *Dear Mr. Henshaw* by Beverly Cleary (Morrow, 1983) to the class. This story describes the relationship a boy has with a famous author.

Make a photocopy of each letter before mailing it. Then help students find out how to locate the addresses of the different publishers.

When students receive responses to their letters, post the photocopy of the original letter and the response on a wall in the classroom reading center for all to see. If any students do not receive responses to their letters, encourage them to try writing to different authors. Explain that many authors receive a great deal of mail and cannot take the time to answer every letter they receive.

If possible, invite a local children's author or illustrator to come to the classroom to discuss his or her work. Help students prepare questions to ask their guest ahead of time. Students may also enjoy a classroom visit from a printer, who can explain how a book is physically made.

Advertisements

Divide the class into groups. Ask each group to come up with a new product for which they will produce a television commercial. The product may be serious or funny.

Advise each group that they will need to split the work among themselves: actors and actresses, director, dialogue writers, and props people. Each student may help in the idea-making and the writing processes.

When the allotted time is up, ask each group to come to the front of the room and dramatize their commercial. Hand out awards for the funniest commercial, the longest and shortest, the most detailed, the most believable, and the commercial with the least mistakes. Try to give each group an award for something unique about their commercial.

If possible, videotape the commercials. Play the tape back at a later point in the year for all to enjoy.

Where Was I?

MATERIALS:

glue
oaktag
crayons or markers
scissors
hole puncher
yarn

DIRECTIONS:

1. Reproduce the bookmarks on page 89 once for each student.
2. Have each student mount the bookmarks on oaktag, color, and cut out.
3. Punch a hole at the top of each bookmark.
4. Have children thread short lengths of yarn through the holes.

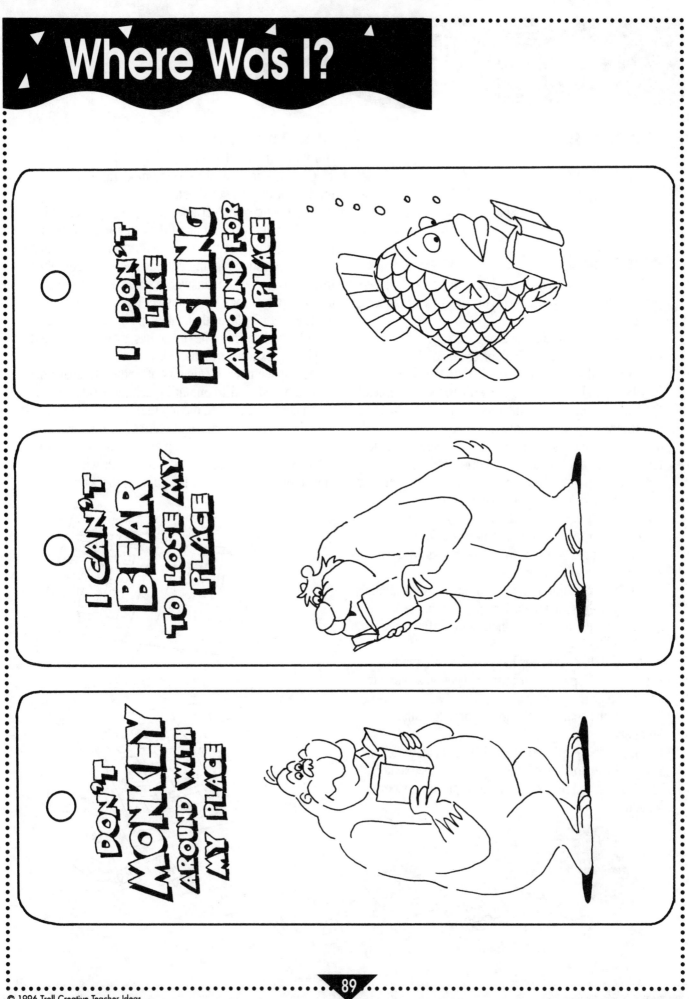

Literary Jeopardy

MATERIALS:

glue
11" x 17" oaktag
sharp blade
11" x 17" white paper
tape

DIRECTIONS:

1. Reproduce the game board pattern on page 91 two times. Mount the game board on an 11" x 17" piece of oaktag, as shown.
2. Using a sharp blade, cut along the solid lines. Discard the rectangular blank pieces, and place the pieces with dollar amounts on them to the side.
3. Place an 11" x 17" piece of white paper underneath the game board, as shown. Tape the paper to the oaktag around the edges to hold it in place.
4. Write the names of various books, literary characters, or other book-related categories in the rectangular box at the top of each column. For example, you may wish to have categories such as "Laura Ingalls," "Medieval Times," "World War II," "African American History," "Native American Culture," and "Hunting Dogs." Be sure to choose books with which all the players are familiar.
5. Under each column, think of four questions about the category. Write the easiest question in the $25 space, and then in order of increasing difficulty to the $100 space.
6. After all the questions have been written in the spaces, make up a master answer sheet on a separate sheet of paper.
7. Cover the spaces with the appropriate dollar amounts.
8. To create a new game with different categories, use a sharp blade to slice off the paper from the oaktag game board and replace with a new piece of paper backing.

HOW TO PLAY:

(for two or more players)

1. Choose one student to be the moderator. Give the moderator the answer sheet.
2. The youngest player goes first. That player chooses the $25 question in one of the categories. If he or she answers it correctly, that player may take another turn and continue playing until answering incorrectly. If the player does not answer the question correctly, the next player may try to answer the question.
3. The second player then takes his or her turn regardless of whether or not he or she has answered the first player's question correctly. Players may only choose the $50 space in each category after the $25 space has been exposed, and so on until reaching $100.
4. To keep track of the money that has been "won," give the appropriate piece of oaktag with the dollar amount written on it to each player each time he or she answers a question correctly. The player with the most money at the end of the game is the winner.

Literary Jeopardy

$25	$25	$25
$50	$50	$50
$75	$75	$75
$100	$100	$100

Reproduce one of the reading and writing awards on pages 93–94 to present to each student after a specific goal has been reached (i.e., reading ten books, or writing an original story).

SUPER READER
AWARD

Presented to _____
Date _____

AUTHOR! AUTHOR!
AWARD

Presented to _____
Date _____

SUPER READER AWARD

Presented to _____
Date _____

AUTHOR! AUTHOR! AWARD

Presented to _____
Date _____

Answers

page 8

1. Pa Ingalls
2. Uncle Peter
3. Mary Ingalls
4. Ma Ingalls
5. Laura Ingalls

page 9

1. A
2. B
3. D
4. B
5. C

page 13

_8_ Wilbur goes to the fair.
_4_ Charlotte and Wilbur meet.
_10_ Charlotte's children come to live with Wilbur.
_1_ Fern saves Wilbur from being killed.
_2_ Wilbur goes to live with the Zuckermans.
_9_ Charlotte lays her eggs.
_5_ Charlotte writes "SOME PIG" in her web.
_7_ Wilbur gets a buttermilk bath.
_6_ Charlotte writes "TERRIFIC" in her web.
_3_ Wilbur escapes from the yard.

page 18

Answers will vary. Possible answers include:
1. She looked as if she were asleep, but I knew she wasn't.
new—something that has not been used before.

2. I cocked my ear to see if I could hear puppies crying, but could hear nothing.
sea—a large body of water.

3. I had lost weight and was as thin as a bean pole.
eye—the part of the body through which we see.

4. You should have seen what I saw one day.
saw—a sharp tool used to cut wood or metal.

5. I kept it up for the rest of the night.
four—a number.

6. I felt so good even my sore hands had stopped hurting.
sew—to make or repair something with a needle and thread.

7. His tail was between his legs and his head was bowed down.
tale—a story.

8. Just before he drew one last sigh, and a feeble thump of his tail, his friendly gray eyes closed forever.
won—finished first in a game or competition.

page 24

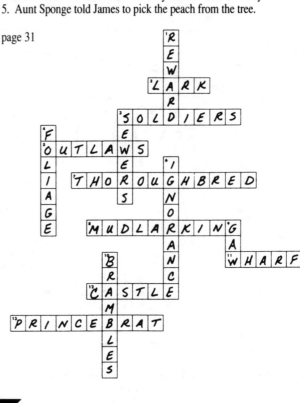

page 27

1. D
2. B
3. E

4. F
5. J
6. C

7. H
8. I
9. G

10. A

page 28

Answers may vary. Possible answers include:
1. James took the silk threads Silkworm and Spider spun and tied them around 502 sea gulls' necks to lift the peach out of the water.
2. The giant peach rolled over Aunt Sponge and Aunt Spiker.
3. James found he was in the home of some giant creatures.
4. James and his friends discover they are in New York City.
5. Aunt Sponge told James to pick the peach from the tree.

page 31

Answers

page 32

Answers may vary. One possibility:

The Whipping Boy is about an orphan named Jemmy who is beaten every time the prince does something wrong. The prince, who is called Prince Brat, makes Jemmy run away with him one night. Their adventures include tricking some villains and being chased through dark sewers.

I recommend The Whipping Boy because it's an exciting book that's fun to read.

page 33

1. The prince's eyes widened and his face blanched white.

2. The king's men were clearly looking for the vanished prince, but when a bear poked its head out the door window the soldiers stepped back and quickly waved the coach on.

3. Jemmy led the way through a tarred forest of wharf pilings and over a derelict river barge.

4. The whipping boy learned to read, write, and do sums.

5. Cutwater wiped his thin, greasy lips with the back of his hand.

6. "I'll swear there are not two more ignorant, cloven-footed blockheads in the land."

7. He felt friendly and trusting.

8. He waved a bamboo pole with long paper streamers fluttering from the tip.

9. Prince Brat sat sullenly on a pile of moldy bed straw.

10. Retreating toward the golden doors, the prince beside him, Jemmy felt a sparkle rise in his eyes.

page 38

1,642 > 1,123	42,611 < 47,905
15,654 < 18,976	8,144 < 12,973
6,467 < 7,433	32,067 < 32,068
9,211 < 9,233	14,896 < 25,956
27,700 < 29,700	56,874 < 58,674

page 39

1. She cupped the insect in her hands and carefully set it free outside.

2. The next morning the Sasaki family joined crowds of people as they visited their shrines.

3. "You tricked me!" he said with a grin. "But I'll do it anyhow."

4. "I just know," he said.

5. He wanted to sleep as long as possible, but like most fourteen-year-old boys, he also loved to eat.

6. Maybe, she dreamed, I will be the best runner in the whole school.

7. As if he knew what was in Sadako's mind, her father said gruffly, "There now, don't worry. After a good night's rest you'll feel fine."

8. She barely heard him say, "It's time to rest. You can make more birds tomorrow."

1. Sadako cupped the insect in Sadako's hands and carefully set the insect free outside.
2. The next morning the Sasaki family joined crowds of people as the people visited the people's shrines.
3. "Sadako tricked Masahiro!" Masahiro said with a grin. "But Masahiro will do the hanging anyhow."
4. "Kenji just knows," Kenji said.
5. Masahiro wanted to sleep as long as possible, but like most fourteen-year-old boys, Masahiro also loved to eat.
6. Maybe, Sadako dreamed, Sadako will be the best runner in the whole school.
7. As if Sadako's father knew what was in Sadako's mind, Sadako's father said gruffly, "There now, don't worry. After a good night's rest Sadako will feel fine."
8. Sadako barely heard the doctor say, "It's time to rest. Sadako can make more birds tomorrow."

page 47

Answers may vary.

Answers

page 50

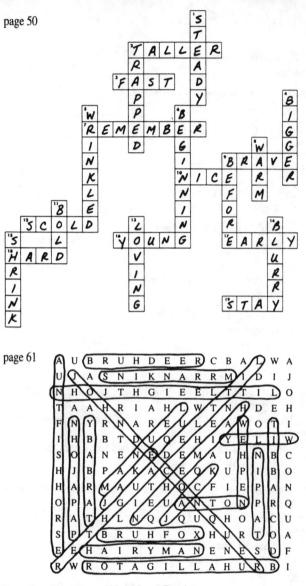

page 61

Two other characters are Manuel and Tappin.

page 63

Answers may vary. Possible answers:

A
A or C
B

page 68

I love talking to Peter, but I'm always afraid of being a nuisance...
He used to think I was unbearable, and I returned the compliment; now
I have changed my opinion, has he changed his too?

page 71

1. 9 x 6 = 54   6. 6 x 12 = 72   11. 4 x 9 = 36
2. 10 x 11 = 110   7. 5 x 11 = 55   12. 3 x 9 = 27
3. 12 x 8 = 96   8. 12 x 12 = 144   13. 12 x 9 = 108
4. 9 x 9 = 81   9. 6 x 10 = 60   14. 11 x 11 = 121
5. 7 x 7 = 49   10. 9 x 8 = 72   15. 7 x 9 = 63

page 72

1. What were her greatest faults? Anger, impatience, stubbornness.
2. His eyes were an oddly bright blue.
3. Or was it a Thing in itself?
4. "What cause have I given you for distrust?" The thin lips curled slightly.
5. There was an air of such ineffable peace and joy all around her that her heart's wild thumping slowed.
6. Aunt Beast stood quietly against the assault.
7. "How extraordinary! I could almost see the atoms rearranging!"
8. It seemed unsubstantial, as though one might almost be able to walk through it.
9. The globe became hazy, cloudy, then shadows began to solidify to clarify, and they were looking into an untidy kitchen with a sink full of unwashed dishes.
10. "Look at something cheerful, do. I can't bear to have you distressed!"
11. "I've heard that clever people often have subnormal children," Meg had once overheard.
12. "You're like Charles Wallace. Your development has to go at its own pace.
13. But she, in all her weakness and foolishness and baseness and nothingness, was incapable of loving IT.
14. With her inefficient flying tackle she landed on him.

Books Used in This Program

Little House in the Big Woods by Laura Ingalls Wilder (HarperTrophy, 1971).

Charlotte's Web by E.B. White (HarperCollins, 1980).

Where the Red Fern Grows by Wilson Rawls (Bantam, 1974).

The Lion, the Witch and the Wardrobe by C.S. Lewis (Macmillan, 1950).

James and the Giant Peach by Roald Dahl (Puffin Books, 1988).

The Whipping Boy by Sid Fleischman (Troll, 1986).

Sadako and the Thousand Paper Cranes by Eleanor Coerr (Dell, 1977).

Island of the Blue Dolphins by Scott O'Dell (Dell, 1960).

How Does it Feel to Be Old? by Norma Farber (Dutton, 1979).

The Indian in the Cupboard by Lynne Reid Banks (Avon, 1980).

The People Could Fly by Virginia Hamilton (Knopf, 1985).

Bunnicula by Deborah and James Howe (Avon, 1979).

Anne Frank: The Diary of a Young Girl by Anne Frank (Pocket Books, 1972).

A Wrinkle in Time by Madeleine L'Engle (Dell, 1962).